THE
COWORKING
REVOLUTION

Four Secrets To Successfully Working For Yourself

BY MATTHEW DUNSTAN

Published by Rising Tide Ventures

Brisbane Queensland Australia

First published in 2015

Rising Tide Ventures

www.risingtideventures.com.au

The Coworking Revolution : Four secrets to successfully
working for yourself / Matthew Dunstan.

ISBN: 9780994164308

Includes bibliographical references.

Subjects: Coworking; Success; Life Skills; Business.

Cover Design by Fiona Boccalatte

Book formatting services by BookCoverCafe.com

Printed in Australia by Griffin Press

As my good friend and mentor once said: Life is like sailing to windward –
you'll have to put in a few tacks before you reach your goal.

Thank you Bruce Lynn for inspiring a vision of success which doesn't follow
the corporate mould. You've taught me that it's possible and even ok to be a
good father and husband as well as a professional manager and leader.

Thank you to my wonderful wife Rachel whose faith allows me to pursue my
dreams – even when they take her to places she wasn't expecting.

To my wonderful boys Alexander and Nicholas, who help me remember what
life is really about on a daily basis.

And thank you to all of the wonderful friends we've made around the world
who have inspired and enriched our lives in ways they don't even realise.

Join the revolution at:
www.risingtideventures.com.au/coworking-revolution

Share your insights, ideas and questions with other entrepreneurs:
www.facebook.com/risingtideventures
Twitter: **@_risingtide**
LinkedIn: **au.linkedin.com/in/matthewdunstan**

TABLE OF CONTENTS

INTRODUCTION

For many, the idea of working from home is an enticing one: 'Escape the treadmill. Move to a new life of freedom, flexible hours and 30 second commutes.' It reads just like a travel brochure!

This is the dream we all have in mind when we start out. We gaze longingly out the window and think "it's time to go for it." And before you know it, you're sketching out business card designs and creating Facebook pages as you sit through yet another 'critical' team meeting.

So you make the jump! You take that bold and courageous step and turn your back on secure employment and regular pay cheques ... but as the freelancer and career entrepreneur knows, the reality is somewhat different.

All the good stuff

Sure your commute is shorter. You get to spend more time with the kids and pick them up from school each day. Yes, you're now able to exercise in the middle of the day and work in the evenings. But there's a cold hard truth about working from home – there's no one else there!

Now at first, this isn't so bad. After all, look how much more productive you are without the interruptions. But after a few days, you start looking for things to do. Your coffee consumption goes up, the washing has never been folded so neatly and your new home office is arranged 'just so'.

Oops, now the bad

After a little while, the house starts getting too quiet. Some music helps, but you really need a change of scene and some social interaction so it's calls to distant friends, trips to the coffee shop and an increasing amount of time on Facebook.

And then the procrastination starts. "I'll get to the book-keeping later.", "Maybe I'll have one more cup of tea and then write that proposal." Day-by-day, our motivation slips until there are some days where you won't have achieved much at all, filling your time by browsing the web or redesigning your business cards for the tenth time.

You are the lone ranger

The reality of working from home is that it's a lonely place. It's isolating; there are a lot of distractions and it can be hard to keep your motivation up. And all typically at a time when you're just starting out and need to be 'on', productive and motivated.

The result for many is a short-lived home career. They return to 'working for the man' and the simpler but servile boss-employee relationship. Even the serial entrepreneur starts to think 'maybe it would be easier…'

Do it better

But wait, this isn't a book about *not* working for yourself! It's just that it needs to be better. But why isn't the home office, the nirvana we dreamt of? What's missing? Ironically, the answer can be found back in the traditional workplace.

Like a form of corporate Darwinism, the modern organisation has evolved into its current form for a reason. It has attributes that make that ecosystem fun, interesting, productive, motivating and successful.

The sad irony is that in turning our back on the corporate office, we've lost four critical ingredients that help make us happy and successful. Four things we weren't able to pack with the photos and extra pens when we walked out:

- the workplace,
- the team,
- the water cooler,
- and your manager!

The power of the ritual

The workplace is designed for focus and productivity and the ritual of going to work helps us make the mental shift from home responsibilities to professional responsibilities. It also helps us leave work behind when we return to our families at the end of the day.

The team is an essential part of the organisation. We accomplish more as a group than as individuals. We rely on the expertise of others to get things done and there's a sense of support and camaraderie that exists when we share wins and failures together.

The power of being social

The water cooler, photocopier or lunchroom is our 'meeting place' giving us a social outlet during the day. Here we perform daily rituals of saying good morning and talking about the weekend. We swap company gossip and celebrate social events like office birthdays, holiday seasons and Friday afternoon drinks. At home, you're slicing that cake for one.

Nooooo!

The final missing ingredient is a manager. "What! That's the whole reason I work for myself!" I hear you shout. Whilst this may be true for some, I'm sure we've all had a manager who we've actually enjoyed working for. Someone who gave us support and direction, who knew when to be hard, to expect more and drive you to do better. Someone who had their eye on the big picture, making sure it's all headed in the right direction.

At home, there is no one doing the annual performance review, no one to give you a kick up the bum when you need it. Perhaps most importantly, no one to hold you accountable for delivering against your goals.

Me is a lonely place

In a nutshell, we love working *for* ourselves, but we'd be more successful and have more fun if we weren't working *by* ourselves. The good news however is that it's possible to have your cake and eat it too. To have a productive workplace, to plug into a team, to be part of a professional social circle and to have that dose of accountability, guidance and mentoring we need to be productive and motivated.

What this book will do for you

In this book, my mission is to give you a new model of self-employment that keeps you flexible and independent but protects you from the debilitating effects of professional isolation. The Coworking Revolution provides a framework for creating the home enterprise.2.0. One where you're still the boss but also part of a dynamic team and where your home office is just the head office.

New work styles are evolving all the time. Until now, the home enterprise hasn't. The coworking trend however presents a new opportunity to work differently and will be a catalyst for transforming the way you and your business operate from home.

Coworking is like a halfway house for the corporate delinquent. It's a *place* and a *style* of working that combines independence and co-dependence. One that allows you to be a soloist, but still play with the orchestra. To be social when you need to and to hold you accountable for delivering the things you say are important.

Coworking restores the four ingredients of success

In this book we'll take an in-depth look at the four missing ingredients and piece by piece, give you a framework which will show you how to:

- Use different workspaces to:
  - 'go to work' at the start of the day and 'come home' again.
  - remove the distractions of home that prevent you from being more productive.

- Co-work with others to:
  - help you stay motivated during the day.
  - find professional, social interaction.
  - share wins and knocks.
  - network more effectively to create growth for one another

- Build a team around you to:
    - ○ create accountability for tasks and goals you set each week.
    - ○ tap into other's expertise to solve business challenges quickly.
    - ○ bounce ideas off each other and get feedback.

This book will help you find a new work style that delivers on the promise of working from home. You'll rediscover your passion, find the support you need for the hard stuff and pursue the dreams you set out for, when you sketched that first business card.

I believe that with the right support and people around you, every entrepreneur can find their measure of success. I wish you the best of luck – I love your courage and spirit of adventure and it's a privilege to join you on the journey.

SECTION 1
THE TYRANNY OF
THE HOME OFFICE

YOU CAN WORK IN YOUR PYJAMAS
BUT SHOULD YOU?

CHAPTER 1

The Glamorous Life of the Latte-preneur (Told Through the Eyes of My Wife)

My wife and I have two school-aged boys. She works for a large national organisation in the city whilst I run a business from home. Each morning we go our separate ways, and I'm sure she feels that she has the raw end of the deal. I think she'd rather be the one staying at home.

She hasn't always been a corporate mum. For the first 10 years Rachel stayed at home and loved the role of mother and homemaker. She's fortunate though to have an employer who provides flexible work hours so she's able to start and get home early so she can be a mother again in the afternoon.

The life of the latte-preneur

At 7am Rachel arrives at work and starts her day. The office is pretty quiet so she gets a lot done. At 7.30am there's often a call home to say good morning, which is really code for 'are you awake, are you dressed for school and has your father fed you yet?' In fairness, the answer is often 'no'. My morning schedule with the boys is a little free flowing … It's a long established rule that my role is that of the 'good time, light-weight dad' and that's how we roll in the mornings.

Eventually she's assured that the kids will make it to school, albeit 10 minutes late. And while she's prioritising her day and organising her to do list, she's secretly wishing she could have a day like mine without priorities or a to do list. That's what it's like being a latte-preneur right?

Um, no

While Rachel's working to deadlines and attending endless meetings, she's picturing me dropping into the coffee shop to read the paper. After all, I am a man of entrepreneurial leisure. In her mind, I'll get home around 10am, have another coffee, make a few phone calls and read my email. Eventually I'll put on some real work clothes because I'm meeting people for lunch. Maybe by 2pm I'll get down to some real work but only until I have to pick the kids up at 2.45pm.

Of course it's not really like this. This story is really about what she misses and what many people assume happens in the home-based career. After all, these perceptions are some of the things I love about working from home. It's just not an accurate portrayal of the average day in the home office.

Contrary what some may believe, I'm not swanning around the house during the day and I'm not spending hours in the cafe or at lunch. Instead, I'm working as hard as I can to keep the business running and the income flowing so I can pay the bills and support my family. If you too work from home, you know the reality is very different to the fantasy.

The Dad's Work-from-Home Job Description

Apparently, when you work from home, one of the things that's supposed to be in the job description is housework. I wasn't aware of this when I was doing my MBA and aspiring to start my own business, but apparently it's true.

It turns out that if you're at home, then you're not really at work. You're available to keep the house and the family running and your performance bonus will suffer if the washing isn't hung out.

I remember when our kids were born, Rachel would call out "Honey, I need to get some things from the store, would you mind Alexander for me?"

"Hang on", I'd reply, "I'm building a corporate empire here. Just because I'm working from home doesn't mean I'm not at work. You have to pretend I'm not really here." Of course that doesn't fly with a mother of two boys under two years old!

Now, the boys are older and at school but I've still not read the job description right. Sometimes the instructions are explicit and she'll leave a note or send me a text (usually several by 8am). Other times the messages are more subtle like leaving a pile of washing by the door. Unfortunately I'm not good with subtle and if I've got a lot on, I'm not good with obvious either.

It seems that I've replaced the interruptions from colleagues with the interruptions of the 'Director of Family Affairs'.

It's ironic that on my best days working from home, I'm slackest around the house and on my least productive days, I'm on top of those jobs. My wife may be happy but my P&L isn't.

Why I work for myself

There are a lot of reasons people work for themselves. For some there is no choice, they have duties at home that make it necessary. For some, they fell into it; maybe it's grown from a hobby. For me, I love to innovate and find my own path so working for myself is really the only option. (Besides, no one else would have me.)

Working from home does have a lot of benefits. I don't put on a suit on every day. I don't spend 90 minutes in traffic. I love being my own boss and not having to put up with megalomaniacs or egotists. At the same time though, I miss the mental stimulation of new ideas and the camaraderie that exists in a team.

Independence

I enjoy the independence – the thought of going back to work for someone else makes me cringe. I love the flexible hours. I often wake at 5am and start working before the kids are up and tend to work again after they go to bed. This gives me the flexibility to exercise, go sailing or even see a movie during the day.

I love being able to choose my work and whom I work with, but that also comes with the burden of finding those clients in the first place. At the end of the day, you still have to pay the bills.

Having the flexibility to see my kids and watch them at after-school sport is also great. I missed a lot of that in the first 10 years. Do I feel a little pressure to be income producing though when I'm sitting there? Yes. I tend to work into the evenings to make up for it.

And what I don't enjoy ...

It's not all fun and frivolity; there are a lot of hard times too. Personally I feel a daily burden to produce an income for my family. Even when I'm hanging out with the kids, there's always a part of my brain that's working out how to find, grow and build that income. Switching off is a lot harder now.

I also don't enjoy having to do some of the tasks that come with running a business. I never aspired to become a bookkeeper or an inside sales rep, but I'm having to take on those roles now. I'm not living the dream when it's time for my tax return and I'm behind in my bookkeeping.

The isolation of working from home isn't much fun either. The reality is that I don't catch up with friends all the time. They're at work. There can be days when the only professional interaction I have is via Facebook.

Living the dream

For those of us who work from home, we know why we do it. We've signed up to create something. We're making a sacrifice, chasing a dream or following our calling.

Some days are wonderful. Every win, large or small is our own. Everything that exists has come about because we created it. The results of our vision, determination and hard work are right there in front of us.

We also know that it can be a pretty tough road. If the highs are higher, then the lows are lower. As a soloist, you need more resilience, more confidence and more faith than most people.

The challenges we face are unique to self-employment because there are a few factors that just naturally work against us. There are features of our new career that act as brakes and inhibitors to our success.

Without really understanding what went wrong, we find that instead of working in a fun, successful and balanced career, we're working longer hours, earning less and not having the fun and excitement we'd intended when we ordered our business cards.

How many of us fell in love with the dream of working from home only to discover an ugly truth: there's no one else there?

We're working longer hours, earning less and not
having the fun and excitement we'd intended
when we ordered our business cards.

Motivation tip: Know your 'Why'. Align your passion to your purpose

You know what you do, but do you know why you do it? What gets you out of bed in the morning? What drove you to start your business? Why do you keep dusting yourself off each time you get knocked down?

Deep down, we all have a fundamental reason for what we're doing. Perhaps it's to create prosperity for your family, perhaps you feel strongly about a cause or feel you were put on this earth to create and inspire.

Understanding your 'why' is an important thing for a soloist for two reasons. Firstly, it connects you with your big picture, the thing that is bigger than you. When things get a little tough, this helps us understand why we're doing it, why we take the knocks and punishment and then get back to work anyway. Because it's something deeply important to us, we can persevere beyond the point when we'd otherwise give up.

The second reason it's important to know your 'why' is that it helps us filter the long list of 'to dos', opportunities and shiny balls that come to our attention. Many entrepreneurs see opportunities everywhere. The danger is that by not focusing your attention somewhere; you don't focus anywhere and then nothing gets done.

By not focusing your attention somewhere; you
don't focus anywhere and nothing gets done.

Microsoft COO, Kevin Turner has a great term for this. He would say, "we need to put all of the wood behind the arrow." It was his way of saying that people needed to be razor focused on the objective and put all of their efforts behind it.

If you understand your 'why' and that becomes your objective, then you can filter in and out all of the possible things you might spend your time on. If they're interesting but not central to your core, then they're not for you. If they are aligned to your purpose, then you're able to integrate them into your activities and make your business or value to the community stronger without fragmenting your attention.

When I first went out on my own, I had so many business opportunities running at the same time that I became exhausted. In one year I'd started a group of swimming schools, a sailing adventure business, partnered with a yacht management group, was a business consultant and started '2nd Base'. They were all aligned to my passions but not necessarily to my purpose (which is to use adventure and entrepreneurship as a catalyst for social and community benefit).

In time (but not before some of the spinning plates had dropped), I let go of the yacht management opportunity and my marketing consulting. Instead I focused on supporting the community of homepreneurs, building swimming communities within schools and teaching sailing as a mechanism for developing families and groups.

Key points

1. There are a lot of stereotypes about home-based business but it's not all lattes and long lunches. If you're considering working for yourself, do your research and really know what's in store for you. Working from home doesn't suit everyone. If you're already working for yourself, don't lose heart; the answer is in the book!
2. Knowing your 'why' is the thing that will pull you through. Read more about knowing your purpose in our Coworking Revolution resources at http://www.risingtideventures. com.au.

Memory bytes

- The work from home job description is the same as the corporate one – without the oversight.
- Working from home should not include doing all the family work during the working day.
- The reality is you're always 'on', the pressure to make money is constant and professional interaction can be limited.
- You become the bookkeeper, sales rep and worker all rolled into one.
- But what you create is down to you, success is owned.
- Focus your attention somewhere, not everywhere.

To do

Visit the Coworking Revolution website on www.risingtideventures.com.au and try these resources:

○ Take our online survey 'is working from home right for me?'
○ Watch the Simon Senick video on knowing your 'Why'.
○ Revisit, write or rewrite your 'why'. Collect pictures that reflect your purpose. Make it into a poster and keep it in the office to inspire your work, day-to-day.

CHAPTER 2

I'm Not Having Fun Yet. Traps of the Home Office

When we tell our friends we work from home, it must seem like an ideal lifestyle. I mean who wouldn't want to trade the commute to town for the commute to the spare room? When my brother calls, the conversation usually starts with "What's Oprah up to, today?" or "sorry, did I just wake you?" And sure, the ability to stay home, work all day in your PJs or go out for coffee anytime you want is one of the office perks, it just comes at a cost.

Distracted, unmotivated?
Self-employment is a tough road and when you work from home it can be even tougher. There are a lot of distractions, it can be hard to get motivated and it can be a little isolating. The home office is not the nirvana that many people think it is.

To live the dream we also need our business to be successful and engaging and still retain a sense of balance. We need to build systems, teams and strategies around us so we're not working in isolation. This is the opportunity that exists through the coworking revolution.

When the honeymoon is over

In the early days, the courage, creativity and passion that people have for their fledgling business is infectious. Their eyes light up and you can just sense the energy within them. They come alive.

The early stages of self-employment though are fragile. Our initial passion and energy can only sustain us so long before the pressure of 'making it' starts to build. If you're lucky enough to hit the ground running with a portfolio of clients and work coming in the door, this certainly helps take the pressure off. But for most those first months and year can be lean and that's when the demons surface.

Plan for the downsides

The impact on these people can be heart breaking. They're stressed and not sleeping. They're worried about their business and their ability to pay the bills. They're shouldering the burden on their own because they don't want to let their family down or seem like a failure in front of their friends. Their family life is impacted, their relationships and their health.

In this state, some will give up their dreams and return to the workforce where it is simpler, more predictable and reliable. Their dreams are lost to them and they again join the queue at the train station.

For others, the drive to be independent is too strong to return so they persevere, but not in a good way. They turn dour, pessimistic and retreat back into themselves. They might binge on work, and go through wild swings of productivity and lethargy. Or be highly social for periods and then hermit-like at other times.

Knowing these risks is a big step toward avoiding them. Know your 'why' and hold to it. Develop professional relationships for support and encouragement. Find a mentor to keep you pointed in the right direction. The coworking blueprint later in this book will show you how to create the relationships you need to stay the course.

Learn to handle the pressure without impacting the family

During sustained times like this, the impact on our physical and mental health can be significant. It can affect your relationships at home and with your friends. There are many stories of couples of who have broken up because of a failed business, letting the stress and pressure build and affect the things that were important to them before they began.

Tim is a marketing consultant who specialises in events. When we recently caught up, I thought I was looking at a different man. He was dour, pessimistic and depressed. His voice, his demeanour and his dress sense all shouted negativity – hardly projecting an image of success that's going to attract clients.

I was worried about him. I didn't realise how low he was though until he handed over his business card, which was now colour printed on thin paper and not even trimmed well. Kevin was on a negative spiral and all because he'd had a little too long between projects.

"Rather than confronting that big elephant, it's
easier to stay in your inbox or Facebook"
— **Robert Gerrish**

The pressure to perform

When you're a soloist, your first job is to get the business running and profitable as soon as possible. If we don't get on the horse and start riding, we're not going to get any place we need to be quickly. The pressure to be income producing is a constant.

Ironically this pressure still doesn't mean we're getting the job done. In fact many people spend a lot of time doing anything but productive, goal oriented work. Sometimes the problem is a lack of skills. Sometimes people lack a strategy or focus for their efforts. Often it relates to procrastination or a nervousness in putting yourself out there.

According to Robert Gerrish, author and founder of *Flying Solo*, this is the number one issue facing small business. "In most cases this is a marketing problem.

They're just not sure whom they want to work with and how to attract them. Rather than confronting that big elephant, it's easier to stay in their inbox or Facebook."

To break the inertia, take a close look at what it is that you're not getting done and ask yourself "does this make me uncomfortable or do I just not like doing it?" If it's something that makes you uncomfortable, take regular small steps you are comfortable with. For example, some people find networking confronting. A simple solution for them is to buddy up and go with a friend.

If it's something you just don't enjoy doing, well the easiest way forward is just to chip away at it. I like to keep 20 minutes a day aside for 'greasing the wheels' of my business. For example, just before lunch, I'll go to my 'maintenance' folder and pull out one of the jobs sitting in there – it might be my bank reconciliation. I spend 20 minutes on it and then put it back in the folder. In small chunks it's not hard to work on and yet little by little, it gets done and doesn't build up (I also get the reward of eating lunch afterwards!).

The motivation-procrastination swing

When you work from home, staying motivated can be a real challenge. It takes a lot of willpower, purpose and drive to get yourself fired up each day. Even if you're able to start the day with speed & enthusiasm, maintaining that during the day can be a challenge.

Sure there are times when you're excited and rearing to go, but like all jobs, there are times when you're just plugging away at the stuff that needs to get done. Without a boss looking over your shoulder, it's pretty easy to keep putting some things off.

For example, I'm a fairly self-motivated person. I work in my passions and love the work that I do. My personal challenge is that when I'm in the office plugging away at things that aren't so inventive or exciting, I'm not in a hurry to get going. It's much easier to procrastinate. Some weeks I don't even look at my to do list because I know there's stuff there that I just don't want to know about.

You're the boss – the downside

By contrast, when you're in a traditional workplace, the issue isn't quite the same. Sure there are times when you don't feel like being there, but you're still going to get things done because that's what's expected of you and that's what you're being paid to do. In the home office, if you don't get things done, there are no bosses pushing you along. No colleagues are staring at you across the partition. There's nothing to drive you back to work.

Whether a start-up or long term soloist, the daily challenge of getting motivated and staying productive is one of the biggest challenges that people face; it's unique to the home office because we lack the people, pressures and deadlines around us to make us productive anyway.

The pressure to always be 'on'

In our home empire, we tend to be much harder on ourselves than an employer would be. If we're not driving towards our objectives or burning through our to do list, we feel as though we're not working as much as we should. The pressure we place on ourselves can be enormous. We feel that we have to have our foot flat to the floor but why is this?

Our work ethic is deeply rooted in our early career programing. We have tapes playing in our head saying 'you have to work hard to succeed' and so we do: early in the morning, late into the evening. Always pushing ahead and feeling a little guilty if we stop to take a break.

The mindset that engenders guilt

For some there's also guilt that comes from working from home. They feel that their friends might not see it as a real job or that they aren't a serious professional anymore. They need to justify their time and demonstrate that they are pulling their weight in the eyes of others.

As a result, we push and push and try to be 'on' all day and often into the evenings. The problem with this is that it leads to burn out, you lose perspective and you're not very effective once you start neglecting your physical and mental health.

Pace yourself

Of course you can't always be 'on'. Every office has ebbs and flows of activity. Sometimes you're working frantically and in high-energy mode and then later that day, you might be operating at a slower mode, researching, replying to emails or meeting a colleague. Back in the office, this is normal, accepted and how we pace ourselves during the day.

At home we forget that it's ok not to be 'on' all day. Varying our pace, intensity and activities is how most people work and helps us keep a little in reserve for when we do need to be 'on'.

Binge working

The pressure to be on all the time can also lead to a dysfunction of the soloist: binge-working. This is where we drive ourselves relentlessly for a period,, perhaps working late into the night for several days and then we crash. Our bodies and our mind stop and shut down. Our motivation falls, our ability to concentrate evaporates and lethargy hits.

This lethargic state carries on for a while but then the emotional panic builds and your inner voice is saying, 'you've got to get back to work.' An inner struggle starts and at the point when guilt exceeds exhaustion we jump straight back into frenetic, extended hours again to make up for lost time— until you crash again.

This cycle of overwork, collapse, guilt and overwork again, is obviously not healthy and a long way from our vision of what working from home is supposed to be like. It all comes back to the pressure to perform versus the inherent characteristics of the home office, which help us procrastinate.

● ●
Home-Work Tip: Maintaining Balance

Many soloists forget to maintain a balance in their lives between work and play, relationships and recreation. We forget to schedule in some downtime and turn off.

Pace yourself, be more consistent in what you do and deliver and be a little easier on yourself. Even if guilt is driving you to work frenetically all day, just varying the type of work and the pace of different tasks will help.

Busy being busy

Susan runs a design and fabrication studio, making decorative screens. She has a separate office at home and a successful business selling her products all over the country. Despite this, she often feels that she has to justify the fact that she's working from home and that she really is working, rather than just shopping, doing her nails or playing the hobbyist mumpreneur.

Of course there's no rational reason why she should feel this way, other than her personal expectations of herself. People don't say to her, "Sure you work from home, but it's not serious is it dear?" but that's the criticism she's defending against.

This feeling doesn't exist if you're a self-employed newsagent or greengrocer. Someone with a shop or office separate from the home has historically communicated a degree of 'serious business' as opposed to the hobbyist who does a little typing from home.

Forget the camouflage

These stereotypes are long-standing and have driven people to compensate or hide the fact that they work from home by having a PO Box for their mail, and installing a phone system to redirect calls. Some hire a virtual office service to take calls and provide a city address for their business cards.

Of course these stereotypes are outdated. Many people the world over work from a home office and it has become common and acceptable to be an independent. There are still the vestiges of these stereotypes but they exist more in your mind than in the customer's or the market's and these are the people that count.

Authenticity is the business theme of the decade and you're not being authentic by trying to appear bigger than you are. Your customers are fine with it and so should you. In fact in many cases, it inspires those people around you. Being relaxed, happy and meeting clients in your favourite cafe is showing them a life that they probably aspire to themselves.

You spend too much time in your head and too much time in front of the screen

"Small businesses, think that if they've got a lot on, you have to stay in front of your monitor. But if you've got a challenge, if you're sitting there agonising, don't. Just put your trainers on and go for a walk. Just get away from your office."
—Robert Gerrish

Most of us understand that spending too much time in front of the computer is a bad thing. It's not great for your eyesight or your posture and just spending that much time 'in your head' hour after hour and day after day isn't great either. Unfortunately for many, working from home means working in front of the computer for the day.

Back at the office, there are things that get you up from the desk and away from the screen: meetings, discussions with colleagues and collaborating with others. There are a number of tasks that take us away from the screen and out of our headspace. We need that too!

It's not difficult to get up from our screens, it's just that many don't. All it takes is a regular break. To stand up, stretch out and make a cup of tea. Sit somewhere for 10 minutes away from your desk and do a different type of work. It will clear your head, give your eyes and neck a well-earned break and let you get back to things with a fresh mind.

Put the screen away at 6pm.

We are surrounded by so many screens, large and small, that even when we've closed the office door, it's still easy to be working or at least distracted by work instead of genuinely spending time with those around us.

Instead of sitting on the couch with your smart phone, leave it in the office and have a small notebook handy instead. It's a great way to capture ideas and to dos without the brain-candy seduction of alerts, popups and status updates waiting for you on your phone.

Home-Work Tip: Work to your Daily Rhythm

We all have times of the day when we are more productive than others. Some for example, are more productive early in the day and others at night. Our daily commitments and obligations also factor into our ability to be productive at different times. Dropping the kids off and picking them up, networking, client meetings, all of these things need to be scheduled into the day. Some of them have to occur at certain times but many can be done at a place and time of our choosing.

To optimise the day and align my natural energy and flow, I've mapped out my own personal daily rhythm of when I do certain tasks well to help work in synergy with my natural daily rhythm.

5am: My creative time is early before breakfast. This is when I'm able to write, strategise and renew my vision and goals. I also like to use this time for inspiration, either reading something exciting, inspiring others or writing a small note of gratitude to a friend or colleague. These things put me in the right frame of mind for the day.

7am-9am: Breakfast and school. I keep this time sacrosanct because it's when the boys and I connect.

9am: After the school run, I like to work on one of my big rocks for the day. My email is off and I'm essentially unreachable until 10.30am. This focused time in the morning helps me move the business agenda forward and work on things that are important. I figure that if I can work on one really important initiative per day, I'm doing better than most.

10.30am-2.30pm is the best time for me to interact with others. This is when I try to schedule my meetings, reply to emails, review social media and make my phone calls.

2.30pm-4pm: This is 'milo meeting' time with the kids when we sit down together and reconnect after school. No work during this time.

4.30pm-6pm: Working through my to do list and planning my priorities for the following day. This is a good time for 'bitsy' work. I don't mind being interrupted; the work is easy to leave and come back to and I can cross off items on my to do list

6pm-8.30pm: Family time. Phone and PC off.

8.30pm: Reading and researching. This is when I like to read up on new topics, trends and ideas.

Not every day runs like this. In fact less than one third of them run like this, but the advantage of knowing my own daily rhythm is that when I do sit at my desk and say, "right, now what will I do next", I can do the type of work I should be doing to conserve my energy, vary my pace and give me some variety.

Mixing up my day with different types of work helps to keep my motivation up. My daily rhythm gives me a structure for varying the type of work and the pace at which I work, all helping me stay energised and pacing myself whilst still getting things done.

Getting the formulae right

Getting the formulae right for home work is critical. None of us entered this life to fail but we also didn't sign up to destroy our relationships, friendships or personal wellbeing either. The problem is that by working on your own, there's the obvious challenge of creating and sustaining a business, but there's also the hidden challenge of keeping yourself going, being positive and productive day-to-day.

The problem isn't that our business is weak or that we're personally failing. The problem is in the environment of the home office and the inherent challenges that come from working alone. I have the greatest admiration for people who work for themselves, but I believe that working by yourself actually limits what you can achieve.

The good news is that this book gives you a portfolio of tools and options to put you on the right path, sustain you during the tough times and surround you with the support and assistance you need to not only be successful but to have a great time doing it and have the work-life balance that you aspire to.

Key points

1. We place a lot of pressure on ourselves to perform, earn and be productive. Some of the pressures are real and ever present. Many are in our head.
2. For some reason we push ourselves harder at home than we did in the office and carry a lot of guilt if we don't live up to our demanding self-expectations.
3. I know that you and your business are great, it's just that you're dealing with an environment and set of pressures most don't have to deal with.
4. Keep a sense of balance in your work, relationships and family. Remember to turn off and disconnect from time to time and regularly immerse yourself in the other roles you have in life.

Memory bytes

- It's easy to get distracted and de-motivated.
- Understand that the reality is different and plan for moments of self-doubt and procrastination – have a failsafe.
- It's much easier to procrastinate at home – so take steps to make yourself accountable.
- You can't always be 'on' so learn to vary your pace and not feel guilty.
- Home office is no longer looked down upon.
- Get out of your head – those are the perceptions of an older generation.
- Take the benefit of a break.
- Find your daily rhythm diary and work to that.

To do

1. Map out your daily rhythm. Lock in the day-to-day commitments you have and then add other elements and types of work to best suit your personal work style. Print it out and put it up on the office wall.
2. Start or join an accountability group. This is a great way to drive productivity and make sure you're getting the important things done. You can find more information on accountability groups on www.risingtideventures.com.au

CHAPTER 3

Hey, Where Are All the People? The Four Critical Ingredients You Left Behind

Like many families, the traditional workplace has its dysfunctions; those things we all know and love to hate. Nothing illustrates this better than Ricky Gervais's comedy 'The Office' where he stumbles through work each day with those colleagues that make us cringe because they're a little too familiar.

The awkward, socially inept boss; the nerdy, creepy guy in accounts; the wallflower on reception and the always inappropriate guy, sitting right next to you. Gross generalisations of course but let's face it, we've all worked with people we wouldn't choose to hang out with on the weekend.

And then there's the politics. The inter-office rivalries, the bitching and back-stabbing, career envy and lunchroom gossip. When we think about all the things we don't like about an office, it's not hard to come up with a very long list. However it's not all bad. And for those who've worked from home for a while, it actually has a few things we miss.

The things we miss:

- The water cooler
- A professional workplace
- Teamwork
- A Manager

In fact, the traditional workplace has four major features that make it a fun, productive and successful environment. Unfortunately for us, these same four ingredients are missing from the home office and without them, work is harder, less productive and our business is less successful than it would be.

The water cooler

The biggest issue but one we rarely admit, is that working for yourself can be lonely. After all, being a solopreneur by definition means there's no one else there. The office on the other hand is inherently more social. Sometimes too social, but professional isolation isn't a problem you find in the workplace.

Even if you're an introvert at heart, it's still possible to have too much of your own company. I remember as a young employee I used to love working from home for the day. There were no interruptions and I could work all day in my pyjamas. When I started my consultancy a few years later, the same was true in the beginning, but little by little I found I missed the company of others.

"Get out and see clients" my friends would say. Well in the early days, there weren't enough of those and you can only badger the same people so often. And besides, you're not as candid with a client as you are with a colleague. What I missed was the water cooler conversations. The spontaneous chats by the photocopier and the shared joke at the lunch table. Of course the traditional office has all of this.

It would really annoy my wife when at the end of the day, I'd be there at the door, waiting like a puppy wagging its tail. "How was your day? What did you do?" I used to talk her ear off when all she really wanted to do was kick her shoes off and sit down. What we're going to show you in this book is how to tap into that same professional social outlet as a homepreneur.

A professional workplace

The lack of separation between home and office is another big challenge for the homepreneur. The 30 second commute to the spare room is certainly convenient but it comes at a cost too. There are a lot of distractions, it's not set up for productivity and many are sharing the space with other things going on at home. As a result, it can be hard to mentally separate home and work when you need to.

Many people have some really creative and funny rituals to start the day. For example, I used to pack my briefcase, walk out the front door, down the side of the house, unlock the side door and put my sign out. This was my 'going to work' ritual to help get me into the zone. Of course it would all come undone when my kids would toddle through with their truck and a piece of toast, wanting to sit on my lap. It's cute when I think of it now, but at the time I missed having an office to go to.

Like it or not, you get more done at a traditional workplace and in a shorter time than we're achieving at home. It's set up to be a productive workspace. Our home office needs to be like that too. This can be a little challenging if you're working from the kitchen table but even if this is you, there are still a range of simple coworking solutions to help you recreate the 'workplace'.

Teamwork

Working on your own for most people also means that they're doing everything themselves. They are the General Manager, the Sales Department, the CFO and the Marketing team. Unfortunately this doesn't mean it all gets done or done well. It also means that the only source of creativity or ideas has to come from either the cat or the person in the mirror.

Many experienced soloists will tell you that they miss having a second opinion, someone to bounce ideas off and check their work. Someone to tell them whether their idea is crazy or they're onto a winner. We miss the opportunity to be creative and collaborate with people. We miss being part of a team.

We also miss having experts around to help us get things done and solve problems in our business. Sometimes they're small issues ones like, "How do I get MailChimp to work?" Sometimes big issues like "My customer wants to cancel their contract". Without a team around us, it comes down to our own skills and experience to get it right.

A manager

A manager or leader plays an important role in keeping you on track. Not only do they give you valuable feedback, but they also give you support when you take a knock, a kick up the bum when you really could have done better and they hold you to account.

I'll admit, there have been times when I could have used some open and honest feedback, someone to tell me I was just plain wrong. Fortunately I get the message in the end, but sometimes, not before it costs me more than I can afford.

In the office, your manager makes sure you don't stray too far from the path, holds you accountable for getting the important things done and has the objectivity and perspective that you just can't have on your own.

The traditional office advantage

So the issue is much deeper than just feeling isolated. The irony is that in turning our backs on the traditional organisation, we actually leave behind the features that can make work fun, productive and successful. We left behind the opportunity to leave home. We lost the professional social outlet that we all need, the team of experts to help us and the people who held us accountable and motivate us to be better.

Every traditional organisation has these four things but as homepreneurs, we don't. And these four attributes are critical. Without them, our productivity slips, we become demotivated and our business aspirations are at risk. Rather than thumbing our nose at the corporate treadmill, we need to recognise the things that do work and bring them into the home office environment. The Coworking Revolution is a blueprint for recreating these four ingredients in our home office.

Key points

1. Though you work for yourself, going it alone is a hard road and the home office doesn't naturally set you up for success.
2. The traditional workplace is a useful model to highlight what's missing in our own home enterprise.
3. To be successful we need to remove the inhibitors to a fun, successful and balanced home enterprise
4. We need our own version of the workplace, the water cooler, the team and a manager.

Memory bytes

O Don't work alone from home, create 'the office'.
O Coworking can supply the four missing ingredients.

CHAPTER 4

I Wish I Could Go to Work

For most people, going to work means actually *going* to work and don't we know it. The lines of traffic, endless red lights, the queues at the station or being crammed like sardines into a bus. It's obviously not much fun and without a doubt, not something you miss when you work from home. Why is it then, many people who do work for themselves, wish they had somewhere else to go?

The simple answer is that for most people, the office is a place to go to and when they're there, it's a place to 'get shit done'. For us, the home office is a place you never leave and a place where *'shit happens'*.

We all love the independence and flexibility of working for ourselves and sure, the 30 second commute to the spare room is a lot better than the 60 minutes of daily road rage, but we're definitely missing out on a few things that help get work done.

Despite now being able to work in creative and interesting places we still need some of the basic office attributes that actually encourage work:

1. An ability to leave home behind.
2. A place where we can concentrate.
3. Somewhere we can be productive.
4. Good office facilities that just work (printers, internet email etc.).
5. A proper place to work (ergonomics of the right desk & chair, a clear workspace etc.).
6. An ability to leave work behind and switch off.

A place to go

Despite loving the idea of not having to 'go to work', it does have its advantages. For many the act of getting dressed and walking out the door is a long standing ritual that helps us transition from home roles into work roles. In fact, many still do this. They imitate this ritual and make a point of getting dressed each day for work as a way of starting the day.

Steve, for example, is a recruitment consultant who works for himself. Each day he gets dressed for work, drives down the road to buy the paper and a coffee and then drives to his office – that happens to be back at home.

Peter and his wife do a similar thing. They get changed for work, drive down to the local cafe for their daily meeting but then come home and change back into casual clothes!

For many, this ritual of getting ready for work and physically leaving is an important start to their day.

The commute we despise also serves a purpose. It allows us to start thinking about our day, organising our priorities and think through meetings and projects we're working on. By the time we get to the office, we're already in work mode. We know what needs to be done and we're ready to begin.

By contrast, when you work in the home office, you miss the ritual completely. In my case, the transition from parent to professional is an abrupt one. I personally find it hard to switch hats quickly and when I sit down at my desk, there's a very good chance I'm still wondering why my 11-year-old thinks it's ok to take butter sandwiches to school. As a result, I sit down and instead of jumping straight in, I'm thinking, "Now, what is it that I'm supposed to be doing today?"

A place to leave behind

The reverse is also true. In my 'old job', the commute home would be my time to decompress, to leave behind the pressures of the workday, play some music and slip out of managerial mode. When I walked back into the house, it was with a smile on my face and I was ready to be Dad again. Is it easy to do this from the home office? Not exactly.

Instead of leaving work and going home, I'm at work and home comes to me in the form of two gorgeous boys who race in the door and tell me about their day. Now I love this, and it's one of the benefits of working from home, but is it fair to them if I'm thinking about work whilst we're sitting down for our daily Milo meeting?

So one of the first things we need to change about our workspace is to turn it into a workplace. We need a way to supplement the home office so that we have a place to go to and a place we can leave behind at the end of the day. But how do we do it?

Coworking – part of the solution

What is coworking? Simply put, it's a style of working where people come together to get work done. It's often in a location such as a shared, open office but also happens in cafes, libraries and serviced offices.

One of the simpler and more direct benefits of coworking is it becomes somewhere you go and somewhere you leave. This is not to say you have to give up on your home office entirely because that's not living the dream either. It's just that you need to have the option of a third place where you can go when you need it.

For example, when my partner and I started a coworking service, I was looking for a place to start the day, somewhere to help me slip out of home mode and straight into a productive space. On the other hand, a friend of mine uses it at the other end of the day. When the kids return from school at 3pm, David heads down to the coworking cafe to finish up the last few hours of the day. This lets him return home with a clean slate and clear head so he can leave work behind for the night.

A place to get things done

The second thing we need from our home office is that it's a place where we can actually get things done.

Back in corporate land, there's no problem with this – it's designed for output and productivity. After all, it's in the boss's best interest to get as much out of you as he or she can in a day, so the environment is generally set up for focus and productivity.

In the traditional workplace, there are minimal distractions and everything just works (or should). You're not spending time fixing the printer or your email because the IT department does that. And then there are those distractions at home that just don't exist. You're not changing the washing over, you're not juggling kids or cleaning up after breakfast. But it's not just the physical characteristics that make it more productive. Mentally, we're in that zone also.

In the workplace, we know that it's head down, bum up, do your work. At home, it's easier to be more casual and relaxed. If you tried this in an office, you'd have colleagues saying, "Hey, pull your weight" or bosses telling you to get back to work. There's a peer pressure and a set of norms that make you productive and discourage distraction.

Again, there are many tips and tricks for daily productivity in the home office and I'd definitely recommend adopting some of the best practises listed at the end of the chapter if you haven't already. What many people find though is that whilst they're successful to a degree, they still take a certain willpower and discipline to adopt and it's pretty easy to just forget about them.

Personal discipline is a necessity when you work for yourself, but just going somewhere that's naturally more conducive to productivity and motivation, is a big help.

Coworking is also a great way to drive your motivation up. Annie, a successful mumpreneur and coach enjoys working from home, but she gets a motivation slump after lunch. She uses coworking then to get back on track before picking up the kids from school.

When you need to get things done, coworking spaces have the great advantage of not being at home so those distractions are removed straight away. You also know you're there for a reason so you just get on with it.

Other people around you are also getting things done, so it mimics the peer pressure and set of norms to be productive. Coworking spaces also have the advantage of great office facilities so things just work and you're not spending time fixing the photocopier.

The benefits of collaboration

When we don't have separation between work and home and the ability to mentally leave and return, the impact is on our families. We run the risk of constantly working and being there but not being present.

The lack of separation from the home is also a productivity killer, which isn't great for business either. There are too many distractions and things take longer to do. It also means that income takes longer to produce and that's not healthy for your business or your state of mind.

What we need is the ability to leave the home office and work elsewhere on a regular basis. By doing so, we're less likely to be distracted, more likely to focus on the jobs that need to get done and find it easier to switch off at the end of the day.

Key points

1. The home office is great for its comfort and convenience but not for productivity and professionalism.
2. We all need a way to separate work from home. Rituals are good. A third place is better.
3. Supplement your home office with a coworking space to give you variety and a place to *get shit done*. Put a regular time in your diary to work elsewhere at least twice a week.
4. Tips for finding, choosing and using a coworking space are found in later chapters of this book.

Memory bytes

- We need basic office attributes; where we can 'leave home', a place to concentrate and get stuff done, facilities and comfort.
- A third place – a coworking environment gives you somewhere to go to and to get things done.
- A corporate office is designed for success – it encourages focus, it decreases distraction and your colleagues have expectations of you.
- Personal discipline is a big part of success.
- Coworking spaces deliver the tools of corporate success.

Home-Work Effectiveness Assessment

The following quiz is a simple tool to highlight inhibitors to successfully working from home as they relate to your personal circumstances. Read each question and give your home office a score out of 5 and your old work environment a score out of 5.

If you haven't started working for yourself yet that's ok. You'll probably have an idea of where you're going to set up and what else will be going on around you. In this case just forecast what you think it will be like and where the challenges might be.

[Score out of 5, where 5 = you strongly agree and 1 = you strongly disagree]

The Work Place Assessment	At home	In the office
Leaving and coming home.		
You begin with a running start each day.		
You're easily able to move into a professional state of mind.		
Your work environment is separate from your home environment.		
You're able to mentally leave work at the end of the day.		
You work into the evenings or during family time.		
Zone of productivity		
You're highly productive each day.		
You accomplish the goals you set out to achieve each week.		
You're able to focus on the task at hand without interruption or distraction.		
Total	A)	B)
Home Office Differential	(A-B)	

If your home office differential is a positive number, you're doing better at home than you were doing back in the office. If it's not, there are some gaps that you probably weren't counting on. These are your personal home work inhibitors. Go back and highlight the biggest difference in your table to see where you need to focus your attention.

Write down three small changes you could make to close the gap.

1. _____

2. _____

3. _____

CHAPTER 5

Hanging Out at the Water Cooler

It might be good for hydration but the water cooler is also the place for gossip, office jokes and discussing the football. Managers might hate it, but it plays an important role in our workday because at heart, we are all social creatures. No matter how much of an introvert you may be, you still need a little social interaction. Unfortunately the home office can be a career of exile.

Just as there are rituals of going to work, there are rituals in how we socialise during a workday. For example:

8.45am *Walk in the door and say good morning to your colleagues. Put your things down, head to the kitchen to make a cup of tea. There, you run into a few others and you chat about your weekend.*

9.30am *You're waiting at the photocopier and have a quick chat with Julie in accounts, asking how end of month is going.*

10.30am *It's Jim's birthday, so everyone gathers round and sings off-key to earn their slice of cake.*

1.00pm *You sit down in the lunchroom and relax with colleagues. You ask about each other's families and talk about what's going on at work.*

2.30pm *Sue walks past and says: "Hey, I'm going down the road for coffee, want to come?"*

The traditional office is an inherently social place but the same is not true for the home office. There are no shared jokes around the photocopier. Not even a friendly wave good morning as you sit down (though the dog is always happy to see you).

Again, the home working environment hasn't turned out to be the nirvana we were expecting. We dreamed of a tropical island existence but it turns out we've actually been marooned. What we need is a way to recreate the daily social interactions that are a regular feature of every other office:

1. Support and encouragement
2. Professional social interaction
3. Connection and creativity
4. Serendipitous conversations
5. Social celebrations and rituals

Support and encouragement

Have you ever had the wind knocked out of your sails? Of course you have. To be a homepreneur you need pretty broad shoulders and deep stores of resilience. There are always going to be days when things aren't going well and the only person there to pick you up and dust you off, is you (I've even had weeks that have been like this).

Customers that cancel, suppliers that don't deliver on time, people who don't pay and that unending pressure of paying the bills and wondering when things will turn the corner. It can make for a pretty tough life, particularly when you look in the rear-view mirror and remember how it used to be.

At the office, if my wife is having a tough day, her girlfriends are there to pick her up. They're the ones who dust her off and take her out for coffee. Her boss is on hand with a dose of encouragement and a reassuring word. And there's not a lot of time to wallow in defeat anyway. There's always a meeting, a deadline or someone waiting for you to finish something. The job itself distracts you and helps you move on.

In the typical organisation there is always someone there to keep your spirits up and help you stay productive. There are people keeping an eye out for you, noticing when things aren't going well and a lot of opportunities to vent your frustrations with people who understand. These are all natural support structures that exist in most offices, just not ours.

The benefits of collaboration

Working without a network of professional support
is like a trapeze artist performing without a net.

The lack of support for home-based professionals is a real risk and something I feel strongly about. We are a group of people who have had the courage to go out on our own, create a job for ourselves and provide work for others. Yet every day we have to put on that armour, prop ourselves up and put ourselves out there without a support crew.

Sure, it's not all rough seas. There are days when you have fantastic wins and things go really well, but there are other days when you're alone in that small boat and the wind and waves are knocking you around. In fact, it's not uncommon to have fair winds and rough seas all in the same day.

As a result, it's that much harder to get motivated, work takes longer and it lacks that spark of creativity and energy you need to put into it. The quality of your work suffers.

What we need around us, are people who understand the challenges of working solo. We need a support crew who know when things aren't going well and lend some support when things get rough. We need opportunities to speak our mind and vent our frustrations. The lack of people and structures to support you at work is a big challenge for the homepreneur. It's enough to make you give up your dream and send you back to the office, but worse, it can lead to significant problems at home and in your relationships. Working without a network of professional support is like a trapeze artist performing without a net.

• •

Motivation Tip: Keep a Success Board in the Office

This is a tip from Andrew Griffiths, author of 'Me Myth' and a number of fantastic books on marketing for small business.

Andrew has a whiteboard in his office and every time he racks up a win, big or small, he writes it up there. On those days when things aren't going well, he turns to the board and right there in front of him is evidence that it's not all going bad.

Each year he wipes it off and starts again. What a great way to keep perspective. Without colleagues around you, it's pretty hard to stand back and see the forest for the trees. A success board might give you that reminder that you've had victories along the way. You sometimes just have to take a deep breath until the next one arrives.

• •

Professional social interaction

Sure we all have friends we can call, meet for coffee and hang out with, but you don't want to become that needy friend or the one always calling for a chat when they're busy trying to get things done. Professional social interaction is different to social interaction. The things we discuss, the aspirations and challenges we share. They are different to those we discuss with our families or friends on the weekend, just as there are social topics we don't share at work.

For example, I might be worried about who my kids are hanging out with at school. My wife and I discuss this in the evening. We would discuss this with close friends on the weekend. But I'm probably not going to bring it up with Bob whilst standing at the photocopier.

The reverse is also true. I might be having a real challenge with a client and at the lunch table, talk about this in detail with Bob. When I get home, I might touch on it in vague terms with my wife, but for all her good intentions, she doesn't know who this client is. She doesn't have the background or context and hasn't dealt with this client daily like my colleagues do.

For professional interaction, we need people who understand what we do, share the same challenges and understand where we're coming from.

So how do soloists find their social interaction? In trying to solve this need, people can become so socially busy that they don't actually get much done. Some are addicted to networking. Helen for example, attends three networking events per week. For others, they spend far too much time on the phone or on Facebook. Some go to their local coffee shop, which is a great way to get out amongst people but the opportunity for social interaction is limited and you're not discussing the intricacies of your business.

How much better would it be if we were able to work alongside people who understood the challenges and excitement of building a business? To share the thrills, spills and exhilaration of creating something new. This is what coworking offers and why people all over the world supplement their home office with a third space.

Professional connection & creativity

One of my biggest challenges working from home, is that there's no one else to bounce ideas off. It's just you, the screen and your personal creativity. In contrast, how often in the office would you hear: "Hey, what do you think about ..."

This exchange and testing of ideas, building one upon another, upon another, goes on all the time. It is an essential part of how we solve problems and come up with creative, innovative solutions. At home, you can only bounce ideas off the person in the mirror for so long. Even the long-term independent worker needs someone to sanity test their work.

When I started my first business, I used to wake up full of motivation in the morning. By mid-morning I was back at pedestrian pace and then by lunch, I was having a motivational slump. Why is this? Because, like the guy who is practising his tennis, I had no one returning the serve. I was putting ideas out there, writing them down, designing them up, adding them to the whiteboard, but getting nothing back.

I used to (and still do) share all my ideas with my wife in the evenings, but I do feel sorry for her. She's just finished her own day and wants to be a Mum again. Instead she's getting bombarded with a day of ideas and "What do you think about this ...?" She's great and tolerates my puppylike enthusiasm well, but I'm sure it must exhaust her too.

To keep our motivation up and to feed our creativity, we need other professionals around who are working on similar things and who can contribute. We need people who can return the serve so we can keep playing the game.

Serendipitous conversation

We've all had those moments where you're worrying away at a problem and out of the blue you meet someone with an idea and bang, you're away. New business opportunities often occur this way too. You'll meet someone at lunch or over drinks and before you know it, you've got an introduction to a new client, an opportunity to work together or they know someone who can help get you past the spot you're stuck on.

This doesn't happen at home because for serendipity to occur, another person needs to be part of the mix. You have to get out into the world.

If I asked you to think of how you got to where you are today, I'm sure part of the answer is going to be hard work, drive and determination. I'm also sure you'll have a few stories about how good luck, chance and serendipity played a role.

In the coworking world, the phrase 'accelerated serendipity' is often bandied around. Now I personally don't like it – I mean, the idea that you can influence and speed up a chance occurrence seems plain silly. But I understand the sentiment. By working around other people, by having more interaction and conversations about what you're working on, you're going to stumble across more opportunity, ideas that send you in a new direction and help get you unstuck.

Serendipity in Action

I'd always wanted to become a sailing instructor and to take people sailing around the world. On my most recent re-entry into the solo-professional world, my wife and I went out to dinner to celebrate the bold new step I was taking and on that very night, we sat next to two other couples. One ran a sailing school and the other ran a sailing adventure business in the Mediterranean. What are the chances! Within four months, I'd started Uncharted Sailing, I was a qualified sailing instructor, had my first charters booked, and was taking people sailing in Turkey and the Caribbean.

Professional celebrations

We all cringe at the stereotypes of the office Christmas party. The colleagues who've had too much to drink, the loud obnoxious guy who becomes even louder and more obnoxious. The awkward boss who is trying to make small talk all night, but just makes everyone uncomfortable. But take that away and whom are you celebrating the holidays with? Do you sit there in your home office with a party hat on?

In Australia, the nation stops for Melbourne Cup day, which is *the* horse race of the year. Ladies and gentlemen alike get dressed up, go out for Melbourne Cup lunches, drink champagne and place a bet. It's a huge social occasion that is typically shared with colleagues but for those people who work for themselves, they often miss this completely.

The same is true for holiday celebrations. The office Christmas party, Easter, even the end of financial year celebration. As soloists, we don't have the opportunity to celebrate in the same way. Are these things important? Well, it might not determine whether or not you're paying the bills this month, but at the time, it does reinforce yet again that you're on your own. It's one more thing detracting from this great adventure of self-employment that we aspire to, but haven't quite got right.

The benefits of collaboration

Even if you like working on your own, you probably didn't count on having quite so much time to yourself. The reality is that a lot of the fun, excitement, creativity and support can only come from working with other people.

Professional isolation is a real danger for the home-based enterprise (and the person running it). Without an outlet for professional social interaction, the hard stuff is harder, you're not having the fun and adventure you aspired to and the success of your business and relationships are at risk.

To enjoy your work, you need other people to enjoy it with. People who can share your highs, support you through the lows, make you laugh and help you stay in touch with the passion, fun and excitement you had when you started out. Without this, there's a real risk of tough times ahead. For some it can lead to depression, for others, a forfeiting of their dreams and a return to their old job. Professional isolation is a major inhibitor to the success of the home enterprise. To overcome it we need daily interaction, which is:

- Based on a professional commonality.
- Beyond superficial small talk.
- With people who know us at least a little and have a genuine interest in us.
- Regular and day-to-day.

Key points

1. Even introverts need support and professional interaction.
2. Social interaction requires more than just saying hello to the guy in the coffee shop, it needs to be on a professional level with others who understand what you're trying to do and what you're dealing with.
3. Creativity, inspiration and serendipity come from others so you need the social opportunity for this to occur.
4. Networking and professional associations provide an outlet for social interaction but coworking is designed to create the opportunity on a day-to-day and less formal basis.

Memory bytes

- Create an environment that supports you, has interaction, creativity opportunities, networking and social connections.
- Set up the support structures an office enjoys for yourself.
- Get out into the world and create those serendipitous conversations.
- Deliberately set up daily interaction with like-minded people.

Home-Work Effectiveness Assessment

Give your home office and your old work environment a score out of 5 each.

If you haven't started working for yourself yet that's ok. Forecast what you think it will be like and where your challenges might be.

[Score out of 5, where 5 = you strongly agree and 1 = you strongly disagree]

The Water Cooler Assessment	At home	In the office
You're around other people most of the day.		
You have others you can bounce ideas off.		
You're able to discuss professional challenges with others easily.		
You're motivated and productive during the day.		
You have a close colleague who supports you when things are rough.		
Your workplace is fun and engaging.		
Total	A)	B)
Home Office Differential	(A-B)	

If your home office differential is a positive number, you're doing better at home than you were doing back in the office. If it's not, there are some gaps that you probably weren't counting on. These are your personal home work inhibitors. Go back and highlight the biggest differences in your scores to see where you need to focus your attention.

Write down three small changes you could make to close the gap.

1. _____

2. _____

3. _____

CHAPTER 6

There's No "I" in Team

It's obvious when you say it, but the soloist by definition doesn't have a team of people around them. We work on our own and do most things ourselves. Of course we knew it would be that way when we set out, but I don't think we understood exactly what that meant and what we would lose as a result.

One of the critical ingredients, natural to an organisation but absent for us, is teamwork. In the last chapter we looked at the absence of people to socialise with. The loss of those who support us at work and lend a hand to get things done is also an issue. Few people really appreciate just how much extra you have to do, how much longer things will take and how much harder it will be when you decide to become a team of one. What we need around us is a team of people who can help fill our skills gap, keep the cogs turning and help us to scale beyond the spare room.

Teamwork

We're all specialists in something. After all, this is typically what we're offering to the market. When you work for yourself though, you need to be the jack-of-all-trades. The Managing Director, the IT department, the CFO, Head of Sales, the marketing department, the office junior and the janitorial staff.

Of course it has to be that way. These things all have to get done and who is going to do them if not you? You can outsource some of them and most people do to a small extent; bookkeeping is a common example. However unless you've reached that financial tipping point, most homepreneurs are keeping an eye on the expenses and doing these things themselves. But it's not a great use of time.

Unfortunately many solopreneurs don't yet have an understanding of how to truly delegate, according to Flying Solo's, Robert Gerrish. "Even though there's never been a better time to delegate, it's amazing how many people just won't let go and think they need to being doing everything themselves."

Organisations thrive because of specialisation and teamwork. They have worked out how the business produces its widget, split those tasks out and give them to specialist teams and organised themselves to work together to deliver the highest quality in the most efficient manner.

For example, if an organisation needs a database created, a customer breakfast organised or an analysis of last month's performance, there are different teams of experts who do these things. They do them quickly and efficiently because it's their specialty. Unlike us, they're not learning or relearning the task each time.

The benefits of collaboration

Given my daily rate, that free customer
database just cost me a lot of money.

Business gets done more effectively when it's based on specialisation and teamwork but at home, you can't be a specialist in everything. We try to muddle through but let me tell you, working away at ten o'clock at night, cursing at the screen, you're not looking like a specialist at anything.

Sure you might be saving a few dollars, but have you ever spent twice as much because the first time you did something it wasn't quite right? How much time do we lose by fumbling through things that we eventually work out, but aren't expert at? How strategically effective are we if large amounts of time is spent on things that take twice as long as it should?

For example, I'm a fairly IT literate guy and my background is in marketing so when it came to setting up my customer database, I thought "sure, I'll spend 90 minutes on it and then get back to client calls and project delivery." Well of course nothing is that simple is it? Even with my knowledge and experience, I still spent the majority of the day working with MailChimp accounts, templates, list structures and data uploads. I was shocked. When my wife came home and asked what I did that day, I said, "I've been mail-chumped."

I had to laugh. Six months earlier I was a highly paid General Manager of a Cloud Computing business, fast-forward and I was the guy fumbling through MailChimp. Given my daily rate, that free customer database just cost me a lot of money.

Now sure, I'd certainly underestimated the scale of the task at hand, but a MailChimp expert would have knocked this over in a quarter of the time. You'll see similar examples everywhere. Amateur bookkeepers spending weeks setting up their online accounting system. Consultants spending weeks setting up their websites. You can spend a whole day designing your business card with a free, online publisher. And no, none of the outcomes will be as a good as a specialist job.

Why do we do it this way?

Why don't we bring in more help? Well, sometimes we don't know we need it. Sometimes it seems easy enough to do it ourselves and sometimes we don't know where to find the help. Often though, it's because of the expense. Particularly before you've crossed the chasm, when you're watching your expenses closely and looking for a return on everything you spend.

Watching the expenses is definitely the right thing to do, but undoubtedly we're not recognising the real cost of fumbling through on our own. I wonder if we'd still make the same decisions in hindsight if we knew what was really involved and we had a reasonable alternative quick to hand. For example, if my buddy was a MailChimp expert and said "that's easy, I can knock that over for you in the morning. It will cost around $150", would I have taken him up on it? Definitely.

Just because we work for ourselves, doesn't mean we should work by ourselves and the cost of fumbling through things shouldn't be measured against how much it would cost to outsource or bring in some help. There's the delayed time to market to consider. How much money are you leaving on the table by not being ready sooner? How much better would it be if you were ready to hang out your sign in six weeks instead of six months?

What we need is a team of people around us who can provide help when we need it. People who can point us in the right direction and lend some expertise as required. People we can learn from, help us get the job done faster, help us save money by not spending it twice and who can save us from having to make quite so many mistakes.

Collaboration

As soloists, we are pitching and selling our work on our own. It's the sole output of our knowledge, creativity and skill. But is that how we want it to be? Do we produce our best work in isolation to others? And where do we get the fresh ideas that help us develop professionally?

In the traditional workplace, the office is like a hive with people and ideas swarming all around. There's always someone saying "hey, have you heard about ...", someone who's found an article, brought back an idea from a seminar or had an epiphany on the way to work. There are a lot of people watching and discussing the trends, sharing and analysing customer feedback. The flow of new ideas, innovation and creativity is constant.

We also have a lot of people checking our work. Whether a physical good like a piece of jewellery, or an intellectual output like a report or audit, in the workplace we produce these things as a team. People are on hand to pick up the occasional mistake or oversight and able to contribute ideas to make things even better.

Aim for collaboration

Collaboration keeps an organisation at the top of its game and is necessary to deliver work that is consistently in touch with what the market needs and where the trends are taking the industry. But on our own, we don't collaborate to anywhere near the same extent.

Now sure, it may be fine to push ahead and do it all on your own. You may be the foremost expert and leading authority in your field. But even if that's the case, how do you stay there? The risk is that we'll be overtaken by other people, other trends or just a different way of doing things.

Even if you're comfortable with your ability to stay at the forefront, where's the sanity check for your work before you deliver it to a client?

The risk is that one day, your client may not like the work you've delivered. Sure they might nod and say thank you, but they may not pick up the phone again because someone else has put something of a higher quality or more innovative approach in front of them.

A common refrain from even the experienced homepreneur is that they just don't have anyone to bounce an idea off or double-check with before they send something out.

A friend of mine runs a successful marketing consultancy. He used to buddy up with another marketing consultant out of town and would often shoot his work across for him to review before sending out to a client. When his buddy moved on though, he missed the ability to pick up the phone and compare notes. He was again having to fly solo and hope that his own ability to sanity check his work was sufficient.

Why do we do it this way?

Why don't we collaborate with others more? Fear of competition is a big contributor. For example, you don't see a lot of solo marketing consultants hanging out together swapping ideas or comparing work. Right or wrong, there's a protective propriety to their ideas that they just don't want to share with others who might compete with them one day.

Even if this isn't you and you're happy to share and compare notes with others from your profession, you don't necessarily have the time available to do it. Often you need a quick answer or review before something goes out. You don't always have the time to send something off and wait for feedback and you don't have someone you can call out to over the partition to quickly check with. At best, you might pick up the phone or send an email but it's not a quick or fluid process.

Joining a group makes collaboration easier

Soloists need to collaborate just as much as anyone, if not more. It's vital to producing quality work and innovation. It helps us stay fresh in the industry and continue to delight our customers.

We need an ecosystem of ideas, creative inputs and quality control that can only come about through collaboration with others on a day-to-day basis rather than of the annual seminar or monthly industry meeting variety.

Coworking, as the name suggests, provides the necessary environment and group dynamic for teamwork and collaboration to exist. Whether physical or virtual, just formally being part of a group gives you the opportunity and permission to ask for and offer help.

Home-Work Motivation Tip: On the really tough days, aim low.

You can't have a great day every day. Whether employee or entrepreneur, everyone has their share of great, average and bad days at work. As a soloist though, we feel these days more keenly than we used to back at the office.

Perhaps it's due to the isolation and the lack of other people and projects to distract you. Perhaps it's the lack of people around to offer support and encouragement. Whatever the cause, you have to remind yourself that it's ok to have an average day and it's also ok to have a bad day. It happens to everyone and just because you're now the master of your own destiny, doesn't mean you're immune to it.

The worst thing you can do though is beat yourself up for it. Many soloists find themselves facing a challenging day and try to push ahead anyway. They fight the current they're obviously working against. This only results in more frustration, more roadblocks and more damage to those around you.

Instead of using that incredible store of entrepreneurial resilience to continue the fight, you're better off recognising the situation for what it is. See the day for what is meant to happen rather than what you'd planned to do. Withdraw, nest and aim low for the day.

People all over the world have days where they don't accomplish much – I'm sure we all remember them ourselves. We needn't be harder on ourselves now, than we were then. Work on something fun and frivolous, get out in the garden or even take a siesta. You'll make up the time later – you always do. So when you're having a bad day, be easy on yourself, aim low and nurture. Things will still be as you left them when you arrive back at work in the morning.

Keeping the cogs of commerce turning

As a soloist, if we're not on deck, then nothing happens. Invoices aren't being raised; the accounts aren't being done; we're not attending networking functions and we are not delivering work to clients. This is obvious. What may be less obvious is that our pipeline of marketing and potential customers has also stalled.

In the just the same way as our delivery stops, so too does our opportunity generation and it's common to hear people talk about going from really busy to really quiet and then back again. This is a common problem for homepreneurs who swing from 100 per cent delivery to 100 per cent prospecting and back again. The issue is that because we're doing it all ourselves, the tap is either on or off. We're not doing these two things simultaneously. What we need is a circle of professionals around us who help to keep an eye on things, even when our eye is off the ball.

Keep the pipeline flowing

An organisation still functions when you're not there. Sure you can't leave it unattended forever, but if a sales person is away or a marketing person is being replaced, the ecosystem of lead generation and sales can still continue.

People are still referring customers; staff are still meeting new prospects around town. Customers are hearing about your work and reading your newsletters. The traditional organisation has the advantage of being able to keep its business development pipeline running at the same time as the delivery function and the absence of someone doesn't stop the whole machine.

As a soloist, what we need is a way for our business activities to continue without us. The solution lies in building collaborations and partnerships. By building an ecosystem of aligned co-workers you have other people watching out for your best interests, even when you're not there.

Home office success takes a team

To have a successful, sustainable and balanced home-based business you need a way to fill your skills gaps, build a team of specialists and a way to scale beyond the spare room in such a way that the cogs of commerce are turning when your focus is elsewhere. Happily, you don't need to do this on your own.

Fortunately there are hundreds of people nearby who are in the same situation and in a position to help. These people are your potential co-workers and the coworking revolution makes it easier for you to team up for mutual success.

Key points

1. You can't be a specialist in everything. Smart people get help to be more efficient.
2. Producing professional, quality outputs is essential. You don't want to seem like an amateur working from home.
3. Your products or services are better and wow your customers more, when you apply more than one brain to the job.
4. Trying to save money by doing it all yourself is false economy. It'll take you longer and cost you more in the end.

Memory bytes

- Choose a team that makes up the shortfall in your skills.
- Organisations thrive because of specialisation – you should strive for this too.
- You'll spend twice as long for a job half as good if you try to do it all yourself.
- You may save money up front, but what's the real cost of you doing a task?
- Your team also helps disseminate ideas, bringing new thinking into the fold.
- You need to find your own collaboration team.
- Sometimes a bad day just happens; don't fight the current; find something else to do and carry on tomorrow.

Home-Work Effectiveness Assessment

Give your home office and your old work environment a score out of five each.

If you haven't started working for yourself yet that's ok. Forecast what you think it will be like and where your challenges might be.

[Score out of 5, where 5 = you strongly agree and 1 = you strongly disagree]

	At home	In the office
Support Crew		
I have days when I'm off my game.		
When I feel flat, I'm able to pick myself up again quickly.		
There are people who provide moral support when I need it.		
Teamwork		
I only work on the things I specialise in.		
I don't spend excessive time working things out.		
I outsource or hand off tasks to others to complete.		
The office runs efficiently.		
Collaboration		
I share ideas with others on a day-to-day basis.		
I find it easy to stay in touch with trends.		
I have people who check and contribute ideas to my work.		
I'm in touch with what my competitors are offering.		
I'm in touch with what my target market is asking for.		
Automated cogs of commerce		
The business continues when I'm away.		
There is a consistent stream of new opportunities.		

	At home	In the office
Others contribute to my pipeline and refer work.		
My workload is consistent and predictable.		
Total	A)	B)
Home Office Differential	(A-B)	

If your home office differential is a positive number, you're doing better at home than you were doing back in the office. If it's not, there are some gaps that you probably weren't counting on. These are your personal home work inhibitors. Go back and highlight the biggest differences in your scores to see where you need to focus your attention.

Write down three small changes you could make to close the gap.

1. _____

2. _____

3. _____

CHAPTER 7

You Can't Manage Yourself

When I tell people that one of the critical ingredients to successfully working from home is their manager, they scoff. "Are you kidding? That turkey is the reason I left!" And I'm not surprised. After all, one of the benefits of working for yourself is that you become your own boss. Independence and autonomy are a big part of deciding to go it alone and for experienced soloists, the idea of working for someone else is an anathema. It's one of the things that keeps us going when sometimes it would be easier just to pack up and go back to 'working for the man'.

However, as we've discussed previously, the traditional workplace has a number of advantages over our backroom venture and one of those is the presence of a manager. More specifically, the influence of someone who can hold us to account, stretch us to perform better and make sure the whole circus is headed in the right direction.

Holding us to account

Tell me, who will hold you to account if things don't get done this week? Generally, the answer is no one. Would it surprise you to know that many soloists get to the end of the week and cross off very few of the big rocks or goals they set for themselves? Of course not, this is probably what your week looks like too.

Few of us set weekly goals but if you are in the minority of those who do and you miss them, nothing happens. You've got a good reason right? You let yourself off the hook, but the important things still don't get done.

Organisations also suffer from sliding deadlines, but not if they're well managed. A good manager has set and agreed goals for the business, team and individual and reviews progress against these regularly.

If you miss a deadline, a good manager will hold you to account so that next time, you'll place the right level of priority and effort towards getting it done. This is near impossible to do on your own.

The benefit of plans and goals

Working at home, days, weeks or even months can drift by without making significant progress towards the things that are important to our business. Just think of how much money you're leaving on the table because your website still hasn't been updated. And you haven't made those prospecting calls or you haven't gotten around to writing that report for your client. I even mentor businesses that aren't getting to their billable work.

When we started '2nd Base', we probably spent the first six months working through business plans, feasibility studies, marketing materials and forecasts. Was it our plan to spend six months on that? Of course not. Our original goal was to launch within three months but time just seemed to slip away. There was always some vital meeting or competing deliverable so it just didn't get done.

It wasn't until we revisited the financial forecast one day and said, "Hey, if we had this business up and running four months ago, look at how much income we'd be generating right now." It wasn't sheep stations, but it was still enough to jolt us into action. Putting a value on our delay: realising the amount we were leaving on the table by not being ready, was a great incentive for placing the right priority on getting things going.

Why do we do it this way?

In the home office, we don't set regular goals or if we do, we're not as hard on ourselves for missing them as someone else might be.

It's also easy to focus on the safe things; write the blog rather than phone a prospect. Do your bookkeeping instead of going to a networking event.

Combine this with a work environment that is inherently distracting and one where it's easy to procrastinate, and you have the perfect storm. It's no wonder that most home-based businesses fail to reach that breakthrough point where you're getting paid what your worth, doing what you love and being recognised for it.

Just because we work for ourselves, doesn't mean we don't need to hold ourselves to account on a daily, weekly and quarterly basis. Because this is hard to do on our own, we need other people or mechanisms that will achieve the same result, ensuring that the things we say are important are given the right level of priority and that they just get done.

This is where the style of coworking plays a role. In this context, it's not about where you're working but whom you're working with and how you work together. In Chapter 12 we show you some simple techniques to drive mutual accountability with your co-workers, for getting the important things done.

● ●

Home-Work Productivity Tip: Proactive Time Management

At the start of the week (Sunday night or Monday morning) I like to revisit the big picture and go through these four simple steps:

1. *I review what I'm trying to achieve over the next three months.*
2. *I ask myself "what I can do next week to move just one step forward on these goals?"*
3. *Taking a leaf out of Stephen Covey's book, I also like to start with the end in mind and fill in the following sentence: "This will be a great week because ... " (I make sure family and fun are included).*
4. *I take my answers from step two and three and put time in the diary for each of them.*

   These four steps at the start of the week set me up for success. They make sure I have a great week; I've been proactive in my business and worked on the things that make a difference. Even if all my plans go to hell, I'll still have accomplished some of the things that are important, rather than spending my time being reactive and running from pillar to post.

● ●

Making us better than we are

Think back to a time early in your career and recall what your performance was like. What were you capable of? How did you interact with others? Did you make any mistakes?

And now imagine what would have happened if you only worked for yourself from that point in time. Would have you developed professionally to where you are today? Would you have the same level of expertise?

There are a number of ways in which we develop professionally, but a big influence comes from the managers, mentors and leaders around us. These are the people who have inspired us to be better, who have given us a kick up the bum when we've let ourselves down and who have guided our development with different learning opportunities and experiences.

Of course there are too many examples of bad leadership and poor management of staff, but somehow if we're not operating at a level we should, we get the message. Whether through peer feedback, conflict, customer comments, annual reviews or just a level of our own personal dissatisfaction, we learn that we need to aim higher.

How to get it out on your own

At home we don't have someone in the other office telling us we could do better. We don't have someone more experienced who knows us and can see where our next opportunity for growth lies. We don't have a manager who is giving us honest feedback, even if we don't want to hear it.

We're missing the influence of someone who has the experience, knowledge and honesty to guide and help us develop professionally. The cost of this missing element is incalculable, but imagine how much better you and your business are capable of being if you had unlimited access to this sort of guidance.

A profound experience I had in my early leadership role in Microsoft came about when I listened to the COO, Kevin Turner, speak on the topic of being hard on your team. He noted that because of the collegiate culture of the organisation, the tendency was for managers to focus on relationships and not give people the bad news or hard feedback when it was required. He argued that we might think we were doing the right thing by these people but in fact, we were doing them a disservice. Without giving them that feedback, where was their incentive to improve, grow and develop beyond where they were today?

As a new manager, this was a revelation for me. I hadn't appreciated that by going easy on them, I wasn't helping to set them up for success in the medium-term. This is not to say that I turned into a draconian scoundrel overnight. Just that when it was necessary to give them frank feedback about their level of performance, I could do so with a clear conscience because I was doing it with their best interests at heart.

What a shame it would be if working for yourself meant that you had also reached the peak of your capabilities. Of course none of us want this, so how do we avoid it?

A mentor, a mirror.

What we need is access to people who can mentor, advise, coach and provide honest feedback. This isn't an easy thing to do when you're a solopreneur but unless you want to stagnate, it's something that must be done.

Leadership

Most of us have had the pleasure of working for, with or near a great leader. Someone who inspires us to be better, who's confident and charismatic manner make them an attractive person to follow. These people have the ability to see the big picture and to communicate a vision that inspires and binds people together enabling all to pursue a common goal without the use of the stick and carrot.

They also have a strategy to get there. They've mapped out a blue print of how to get from where they are today, to where they want to be over a three year horizon. And then during the year, they have the ability to step out of the detail, assess progress and make course corrections when things aren't going to plan. They have a talent for steering the ship. Again, as a soloist, the person steering the ship is you and this is almost impossible when you're also the person bailing furiously to stop the boat sinking.

The organisation also has rhythms and processes that reinforce their ability to be a strategic organisation. Annual planning off sites, budget setting processes, quarterly and annual reporting to stakeholders, management reporting and performance reviews. All of these things are processes that help keep the organisation, its people and performance aligned to the goals and strategies of the business.

Give yourself a vision

Without having a strategic influence in the business, we drift from one opportunity to the next and our chance of reaching our goals diminishes greatly. No business can afford to stagnate and as entrepreneurs, it's not in our nature anyway, but without the guiding hand on the tiller, that's the risk we run. The risk that in one year or five, we'll still be doing the same things and lamenting the fact that nothing's changed. And for those who are still pushing towards the breakthrough point of success, they won't get there. They'll still be up at 11pm doing invoicing in five years' time.

I remember coaching some close friends who run a training business. They were super organised and very good at what they did. They had processes for everything and their standard of work was as good as any you'd find in the market.

They also knew that the business relied on them and seven years on, they were a little concerned for their ability to step away from the business, or the ability to just take a holiday. They were so busy delivering that they found it hard to step back for long enough to revisit their vision for the business let alone craft a strategy that would help them arrive at a new place.

Of course they aren't alone in this. Very few homepreneurs have a written vision, goals and strategy for their business.

Document your vision, goals and strategy

Knowing that these things are best practise, why don't we do them? Well there are many reasons. Firstly, not everyone is a master strategist, so it's not necessarily everyone's talent. Also, very few people have had any training in setting long-term goals and strategies and that can make it hard too.

Even for those who do have capabilities at this level, just taking the time away from growing or delivering business makes it difficult to get the necessary perspective. It's just hard to see the forest for the trees.

We also lack any process related imperative to do this, to assess and report against progress towards our objective. Because of our autonomy, there's no quarterly reporting to the board, no planning offsite or annual forecasting and there's no one doing our performance review.

What we need is a way to give ourselves time to step back and answer these questions and a process that makes it easy to review our progress against these periodically. Again, the answer to this lies in our coworking strategy because all of your co-workers have the same needs.

Simple ideas such as holding a joint planning session with your co-workers can go a long way. It allows you to carve out time to work on your business rather than in it and gives you the input and ideas to help refine and strengthen your plan for the year. We take a closer look at this and other ideas to drive strategy and accountability, in chapter 13.

Key points

1. You need to know your purpose, goals and how you're going to get there. Without direction, meaning and a plan, you'll never move to where you want to be.
2. You need to be working on the right things and getting the right stuff done. Accountability is hard to enforce on your own and your home office has too many opportunities for you to procrastinate and get distracted.
3. You need expertise and perspective to take you and your business to the next level. Sure you might be able to do it on your own but it will be a longer, less direct route and you still may not aim high enough.

Memory bytes

- We all need a manager ... but the homepreneur can choose who that will be.
- It's easy to do the simple stuff without a 'boss' to make you do the hard stuff that also needs doing.
- Source a mentor for your business and your future growth.
- Use the strategy and vision processes a corporate uses to deliver on your goals.

Home-Work Effectiveness Assessment

Give your home office and your old work environment a score out of five each.

If you haven't started working for yourself yet that's okay. Forecast what you think it will be like and where your challenges might be.

[Score out of 5, where 5 = you strongly agree and 1 = you strongly disagree]

	At home	In the office
Accountability		
I work to a quarterly goal and plan.		
I set goals each week.		
I share those goals with others.		
I accomplish those goals each week.		
I'm held accountable for achieving these goals no matter what.		
I'm driven to completing what I commit to do.		
Professional Development		
I invest in my own professional development.		
I receive feedback on my performance.		
I know where my weaknesses lie and where I need to improve.		
Leadership		
You have a vision for the business that you've documented.		
You've set goals for the business that are specific, measurable and time bound.		

	At home	In the office
You have a strategy or road map for how you're going to get there.		
You assess your progress against these goals at least quarterly.		
You have monthly, weekly and daily objectives that align to your plan.		
Total	A)	B)
Home Office Differential	(A-B)	

If your home office differential is a positive number, you're doing better at home than you were doing back in the office. If it's not, there are some gaps that you probably weren't counting on. These are your personal home work inhibitors. Go back and highlight the biggest differences in your scores to see where you need to focus your attention.

Write down three small changes you could make to close the gap.

1. _____

2. _____

3. _____

SECTION 2
THE COWORKING
REVOLUTION

HOW TO WORK FOR YOURSELF
WITHOUT WORKING BY YOURSELF.

CHAPTER 8

The Coworking Revolution

Co-what?

There are very few, completely new ideas – just an evolution of an existing idea. Coworking is one of those. It's what you're doing when you work alongside someone, but not in an office. You see examples of this all the time in coffee shops and libraries all over the world. But it's actually been going on much longer than that.

Remember the Boston Tea party or the Café Hauses of Europe in the late 19th century? Here, groups of people got together in a common place to work and collaborate. Now wind forward 100 years and the same things are going on in Starbucks today. It's just that we've added wi-fi, it's more gender neutral and our coffees have fancy names.

The Coworking Revolution

Of course there are some big differences between the Café Hause and today's coworking cafe. Today you can co-work in a serviced office, a museum and even a 'Google-esque' coworking centre complete with bean bags & funky wall paper. There are coworking centres for creatives, spaces for consultants and team desks for small groups of start-ups and entrepreneurs.

In 2013 there were an estimated 110,000 people coworking[1] and these were just the members of formal coworking centres. Amazingly, this number has doubled every year over the last three years.

---

1   http://www.deskmag.com/en/2500-coworking-spaces-4-5-per-day-741

Every day across the world there are four to five new coworking centres opening their doors and they can be found in 81 countries around the world. Today there are online magazines, global surveys and even international coworking conferences.

But the revolution continues. With the explosion in online professional groups, tools and services, people are increasingly forming teams and working together virtually. Where we once needed to leave the home office to interact and collaborate, it's now possible to work together online. Tools such as Skype and Google hangouts allow us find and interact with others. Services such as Elance and Fiverr make it possible to build our team and work together.

Coworking success stories

Harry Lin, CEO of Lottay, an online gifting service, interviewed by Chris Cameron, readwrite.com[2]:

"The thing about a startup is that you're always under-resourced; you never have enough people, ... so the more you can make out of less, the better off you are, the faster you can go, and a startup is all about speed."

We would come up with a problem or a hurdle we couldn't get over and we would just shout out, "Hey has anyone ever done this with a library?" and some guy would jump up and say, "Yeah, I've done that!" Voila! Problem solved. And that would happen all the time. So we were getting the benefit of this very open, huge brain trust ... even though, technically speaking, we were just paying for the two guys."

If possible, I would not do the 'in your basement' or 'in your garage by yourself'. Those are the legendary stories we like to hear about, but I think the majority of successful start-ups have had some kind of coworking environment. I worked for nine years in the Bay area and I know that while there are official incubators, there are also these offices where nine out of the

---

2   http://readwrite.com/2010/03/10/entrepreneurs-view-on-benefits-of-coworking

ten companies there are high-tech companies. Being with other people who are doing the same thing is hugely beneficial.

There will be 100 problems to solve every week. I can guarantee you that at least 75 of those problems have already been experienced and solved by someone else. That's the problem with being in a garage or a bedroom by yourself; you'll probably end up trying to solve those 75 problems yourself. When you're co-located and coworking with other entrepreneurs, you can share. "Oh, you've got that problem? I've had that problem, and here's the solution." You can benefit from their learnings and not have to reinvent the wheel, which saves you a lot of time.

Lydia Dishman, FastCompany.com[3]:

Fun. Friendly. Inspiring. Collaborative. Productive. If you wouldn't define your workplace with any or all of those terms, you may have to ditch your desk and take a seat at a coworking space near you. Even if you aren't an entrepreneur or freelancer, the benefits of coworking, according to Deskmag's Annual Global Coworking Survey, are pretty hard to ignore:

- 71% report a boost in creativity since joining a coworking space.
- 62% said their standard of work had improved in a coworking space.
- Almost 90% of co-workers report an increase in self-confidence.
- 70% of co-workers feel healthier than they did working in a traditional office.
- Between a third and half of all workers are flexible and mobile.
- 64% of co-workers are better able to complete tasks on time.

Dodd Caldwell, founder of Loft Resumes and MoonClerk, has been coworking for two and a half years in Greenville, S.C. Most recently, he's sharing space with other start-ups at Iron Yard. "We're a pretty curated coworking space, so even though we're made up of different companies, we're all fairly kindred spirits," Caldwell asserts. By running his small businesses in a curated coworking space, he says, "I get the advantages of the culture of

---

3   http://www.fastcompany.com/3004788/future-coworking-and-why-it-will-give-your-business-huge-edge

a medium-size business without having to deal with most of the downsides that come with it, like bureaucracy."

So why doesn't everyone co-work?

Of course there's never a one size fits all and whilst coworking is undoubtedly good for business, there are some aspects that make coworking difficult for some.

The biggest issue for many is the expense. A coworking centre might charge you up to $650 per month to be a member. This is a lot of money for the average homepreneur and in the early days you'd probably be better off spending that on marketing.

Coworking in cafes is a cheaper alternative and has become popular (though not with the cafe owners). Here though, noise, lack of privacy and ergonomics don't always work in your favour.

Some can't co-work because there isn't a space nearby. The average co-worker travels 20 minutes to their coworking space. If you're used to a two hour commute, this is a big improvement, but it's still not anything on the 30 seconds commute from the kitchen to the home office.

Another reason you might find is that you're actually too busy to get value out of your coworking membership. Let's face it, if it's costing you several hundred dollars per month, you want to spend a bit of time there. However some people don't want to work there all day or the nature of their work has them travelling which leads me to the final catch, you may be mobile, but your coworking centre isn't.

It's not about the space, it's about the people and what you do together.

Now don't let these things discourage you. There are people coworking all over the place. They just find a style of coworking that suits them, their location and their budget. The important point to note though is that the coworking revolution isn't just about where you work. We need to think beyond the space, the bean bag and the quality of the coffee. We also need to find ways to recreate the teamwork, collaboration, motivation, support and accountability we don't have. In short, it's not about the space, it's about the people and what you do together.

So how do we take advantage of the coworking revolution to turbo-charge our home-based careers? We need to look at coworking in its broadest sense and use it as a catalyst for recreating those critical elements that every fun, productive and successful organisation has, except ours: the workplace, the water cooler, the team and the manager.

Over the next few chapters we'll drill into the coworking catalyst framework that will give you a blueprint for evolving your work style and home-based business into the home enterprise 2.0.

Key points

1. Coworking is a fast growing, world-wide trend designed to give independent workers a third space when they need to get out of the home office.
2. More than a space, it's also a style of working. It presents a solution to the exile of the home office and a way for people to collaborate with other homepreneurs.
3. Beyond the face-to-face interaction, modern technologies, tools and services now extend the opportunity to co-work with people virtually and across borders.
4. With an ever increasing number of people trading traditional employment for self-employment, the coworking revolution is the answer to retaining the fun, structure and support they are used to.

Memory bytes

○ Coworking is a new way of working, with four to five centres opening their doors every day.
○ Good news case studies abound.
○ People who co-work report an increase in their health, self-confidence, quality of their work and productivity.

CHAPTER 9

The Coworking Blueprint. Recreating the Four Critical Ingredients to Home Enterprise Success

As we've said, when we turned our back on traditional employment, we also unwittingly turned our back on the four ingredients that make work fun, rewarding and successful. We left behind a productive workplace, professional social interaction, a team of people to help us get things done and a manager to provide guidance, perspective and accountability.

Coworking can be used as a catalyst for recreating these four ingredients. As a space, it can recreate the workplace and the social outlet you've lost. As a work style, it can allow you to find the team and those management influences that help your business grow and succeed. Combined with online tools and services, you can have these ingredients in any place and in any measure you like.

The ingredients of coworking have always existed in some form and yet people haven't used them for their own benefit. Like baking, the ingredients alone don't make a cake. It's not enough for all of these possibilities to exist. You have to have a structure and format to combine them so as that it becomes a natural way of working.

In this section of the book, we map out a blueprint to recreate and combine each of the four ingredients in such a way that they become a natural part of your home working style. We delve into each of the four ingredients, look at how people use coworking spaces and styles to best effect and examine options to help you choose and combine solutions that best suit your needs.

Coworking revolution blueprint

The four components to the coworking blueprint are aligned to the four missing ingredients in our home office. In each phase of the blueprint, we draw out specific success characteristics that feed into and make the next phase possible. An overview of the coworking blueprint is as follows:

Step 1: Working in the right place

The first step is to find a productive workplace that addresses the natural inhibitors of the home office and suits your location, style and budget. It looks at strategies for supplementing the home office rather than replacing it, and creating the opportunity for variety and flexibility.

Separating work from home and creating an additional focused and productive environment is the fundamental first step in the Coworking Revolution blueprint. When you've successfully completed this step, your personal productivity and motivation take an immediate leap in the right direction. It also unlocks the value of the next step in the process.

Step 2: Spend time with the right people - the water cooler

Spending time in the right place, you'll now find it easier to spend time with the right people. Those who understand what you're trying to do and the challenges of being a solopreneur. This is the next critical step to unlocking the value of coworking.

The third space you've found, joined or created is your outlet for professional social interaction. The people you meet and now work alongside are your new co-workers (with the added benefit that if you don't like them, you can always leave!). When you've successfully implemented the strategies of this phase in the blueprint, you'll never again say that working for yourself is isolating.

These first two steps are about fixing the FUNdamentals. They provide you with the opportunity to break out of the four walls of the home office and spend time in a more social environment. This is where most co-workers stop but shouldn't, because though you have filled your social needs, it doesn't mean you've filled your bank account. You now need to leverage these two ingredients to build the skills, scale and success in your business.

89

Step 3: Build a team

Now that you have a place to work and people to work with, you've started to build a pool of people around you with the skills and abilities to help you grow.

In this step of the blueprint, we focus on different ways to bring these people together into a more structured collaboration. We show you how to identify who you need, where to find them and how to work together for mutual success.

At this stage of the process, you're now starting to unlock the full potential of coworking. You've moved beyond the hygiene factors of 'get me out of the home office' and now focusing on using coworking space and work style to grow your business.

Step 4: Creating an advisory board – Your manager

The final step in the coworking revolution blueprint is to recreate the accountability, guidance and perspective that for most people comes from their manager but for us, needs to come from elsewhere.

This final and critical step is the capstone of the blueprint and has the greatest opportunity to unlock the value in your home enterprise. It enables you to be strategic in your business, drive its development forward and tap into experience and expertise to take things to the next level.

In this step we show you how to recreate the management team, how to find and select people to work with and how to use coworking tools to facilitate the process.

The Coworking Revolution Blueprint is a logical series of steps that take you through four phases of transforming your business from a one-man operation in the spare room, to a fun and successful home enterprise. It identifies different approaches to implementing each of these phases, options to suit different work styles and needs and provides tools and tips to make the style of coworking a natural part of your daily routine.

Key points

1. It's not just about the space. It's about the people and what you do together.
2. Coworking needs to be your style of work. It's how you combine spaces, groups and tools to create a flexible and collaborative work environment.
3. The Coworking Revolution blueprint is a four step method for recreating a productive workplace, spending time with the right people and through these, building a team and group of advisors to help your business succeed.
4. Used in the right way, coworking strategies act as a catalyst for re-inventing the workplace, the water cooler, the team and the manager.
5. By successfully implementing the coworking blueprint, you'll create the fun, collaborative and successful home enterprise you always aspired to.

Memory bytes

- Separate work from home.
- Find the right people.
- Build your team.
- Create an advisory board.

CHAPTER 10

The Workplace: Your Home Office is Just Your Head Office

1st Inhibitor to home-work success: working in the wrong places

- Lack of mental separation between home and work.
- A distracting and unproductive environment.
- Lack of quality office facilities.
- An amateur environment leading to an amateur mindset.

Coworking blueprint:

Step 1: Find your coworking space.
Step 2: Plug into your community.
Step 3: Build a team.
Step 4: Create an advisory board.

To recap, what does the corporate office have that the home office doesn't? It's a place to go to and when you're there, it's a place to get shit done. In contrast, the home office is a place you never leave and it's a place where shit happens.

When we start out, our vision for the ideal home-based career often looks like this:

- We don't have to commute.
- We can work when we want.
- It's a creative, attractive space where we get our best work done.
- It can be a casual, relaxed and creative space.

What we need though is:

- A place where we can concentrate.
- Somewhere we can be productive.
- An ability to leave home behind.
- An ability to leave work behind and return home.
- Good office facilities that just work (printers, internet email etc.).
- A proper place to work (ergonomics of the right desk & chair, a clear workspace etc.).

Coworking blueprint part 1: Creating your new workplace

A place to go and a place to leave

So one of the first things we need to change about our workplace is that we need a way to supplement the home office so that we have a place to go to; a place we can leave behind at the end of the day. But how do we do it?

This is one of the simpler and more direct benefits of coworking because it is somewhere you go and somewhere you leave. This is not to say you have to give up on your home office entirely because that's not living the dream either. You just need to have the option of a third place where you can go to when you need it.

A place to get shit done

The second thing we need from our home office is that it's a place where we can actually 'get shit done.'

Back in corporate land, there's no problem with this – it's designed for output and productivity. After all, it's in the boss's best interest to get as much out of you as he can in a day, so the environment is generally set up for focus and productivity.

In the traditional workplace, there are minimal distractions and everything just works (or should). You're not spending time fixing the printer or your email because the IT department does that. And then there are those distractions at home that just don't exist. You're not changing the washing over; you're not juggling kids or cleaning up after breakfast. But it's not just the physical characteristics that make it more productive. Mentally, we're in that zone also.

In the workplace, we know that it's head down, bum up, do your work. At home, it's easier to be more casual and relaxed. If you tried this in an office, you'd have colleagues saying, "hey, pull your weight" or bosses telling you to get back to work. There's a peer pressure and a set of norms that make you productive and discourage distraction.

So the corporate office has three characteristics that help us be more productive. Firstly, it's setup to encourage focus. Secondly, its absence of distractions and thirdly, the expectation of your colleagues that that's what you're there to do. But how do we re-create some of these features to help us get our own shit done?

The Productivity App

Greg, who has always worked for himself, has two anti-procrastination apps on his PC to help him stay focused but they're completely useless. Why? Because he turns them off when they start to annoy him.

Personal discipline is a necessity when you work for yourself, but just going somewhere more conducive to productivity and motivation helps. When you need to get shit done, coworking spaces have the great advantage of not being at home, so those distractions are removed straight away. You also know you're there for a reason so you just get on with it. Other people around you are also getting their shit done, so it mimics the peer pressure and set of norms to be productive. If you use a coworking centre, it has the advantage of great office facilities so things just work and you're not spending time fixing the photocopier.

Coworking is also a great way to increase your motivation. Amy, a successful mumpreneur and confidence coach enjoys working from home, but she gets a motivation slump after lunch. She uses coworking then to get back on track before picking up the kids from school.

Your coworking space options

Coworking spaces vary in their style, location, facilities and cost. At one end of the spectrum you have the local library. At the other, you have a serviced office and in the middle there are lots of variations on the theme.

In choosing a coworking solution you should start by thinking through what you need:

1. Do you need a dedicated workspace or just a break from the home office?
2. Do you need privacy for your work, a quiet place for phone calls and a dedicated meeting room?
3. When do you need it? Is it during normal business hours or do you need it after-hours?
4. Are there other distractions at home that make it hard to be productive there (e.g.: kids at home).
5. Do you need full office facilities such as a printer, internet and kitchen or would you just use those at home?
6. Does the workspace need to be an attractive one or is a more utilitarian space fine?

And now, considering those questions, answer this:

"In an ideal world and if I could have anything I want, I would spend ___ per cent of my time in my home office and ___ per cent of my time working somewhere else."

The answers to these questions will determine what kind of coworking you need. A quick review of the types and features of coworking options follows:

	Library	Cafe	Coworking Cafe	Coworking Centre	Shared office	Serviced Office
Dedicated workspace				x	x	x
Privacy						x
Meeting rooms				x	x	x
Extended hours		x	x	x	x	x
Lack of noise & distractions	x				x	x
Basic facilities (internet & desk)	x	x	x			
Full office facilities			x	x	x	x
Attractive location	x	x	x	x		
Mobility & convenience	x	x				
Opportunities to collaborate			x	x	x	

Library & museum

Before the advent of the laptop, the internet and the modern cafe culture, the library was the place where people would go to work. There were desks set up for the purpose and you'd find people from all walks of life doing the same thing. These days, fewer people go to the library to work but it's still a viable option for some.

Robert Gerrish, founder of Flying Solo used his local library to write his book[4]. "This is really before coworking spaces came about but at that time it was the discipline of being in a different space. I didn't commune with other

---

4   Flying Solo: How To Go It Alone in Business Revisited by Robert Gerrish, Sam Leader and Peter Crocker (Feb 6, 2012)

people, but I just had other studious people around me and I found it really useful when it came to focusing on my writing."

The pros: there's generally one nearby, there's always room, it's quiet, it has internet and a desk and it's free to use.

The cons: It can be a little utilitarian and uninspiring. You'll still be working on your own because conversation is discouraged. There's often printing but no other office facilities and you can't take phone calls without the grey haired librarian glaring at you over the top of her tortoise shells.

In short, the library suits people who need a place to work for short periods of time. If you only need to escape the home office during school holidays or after the kids come home, this isn't a bad option and won't affect the budget.

Cafe

Cafes have been a favourite of the home worker for over a decade now. Ever since Starbucks introduced wi-fi, people have been dropping into their local cafe to work.

The pros: Great coffee, good location and vibe, there's one on every corner and you'll find others doing a similar thing.

The cons: The noise can be a little distracting but on the positive side, it tends to give you a level of white noise for private discussions. The owner might not appreciate you taking up that table for too long so you might find you're buying and drinking coffee more than you should.

In short, if all you need is a change of scene or somewhere a little more social for a short period, the cafe will probably suit you. You can optimise the experience by choosing cafes that are quieter, visiting them outside of rush hours and making sure you pay your way with a regular purchase. Even then you'll still need to make sure you've got an understanding proprietor. When setting up '2nd

Base', we were looking for coworking cafe partners in one particular town but couldn't find a cafe that had internet. When we asked one of the waiters why this was, he said, "No one in this area does because if we did, people would come in here and work." Not all cafes are open to coworking.

Starbucks Discourages Laptop Hobos

In 2010 some Starbucks stores began blocking the use of electric outlets as a means of creating more space for their non-working clientele. It seems that these customers were complaining that there was nowhere to sit and enjoy their coffee because all of the available desks were being taken up by co-workers.

Source: CNBC interview with Starbucks spokesman Alan Hilowitz

Coworking cafes

These are a relatively new addition to the coworking scene and are cafes and hotels that make a portion of their space available to co-workers. For example, LiquidSpace partnered with Marriott and Westin to make their hotels available for coworking. They provide internet and printing and of course are happy to sell you coffee and lunch whilst you're there.

The pros: Reasonable facilities, space and noise levels to get things done.

The cons: There's a membership or a day rate to use these facilities, which you need to factor in.

In short, coworking cafes are a good solution for people who don't want to commit to a serviced office but still want somewhere to collaborate and work with permission.

Coworking Centres

The pros: Good blend of open, collaborative spaces and office facilities.

The cons: Starting to get a little pricier. Your monthly fee is going to be a few hundred or more so it's got to be something you need. It's also not necessarily around the corner so there may be a commute involved.

In short: Great for people who definitely need a dedicated workplace, which perhaps isn't possible at home. It's also good for those people who have reached a level of success in their business where it's now affordable and they can pay to work full-time in a more social setting:

Shared and serviced offices

These solutions have been around long before coworking became trendy, though companies like Liquid Space have made it more flexible and convenient than in the past. In essence, you're paying to be in a formal office environment either by renting your own serviced office, or the corner of someone else's office (share office space).

The pros: Definitely has all of the features of the traditional workplace. Facilities, free from distractions, internet & kitchen. It also has the benefits of a formal office address, reception and meeting rooms.

The cons: It's at the top end of what you'll pay and it's not always the most attractive place to spend time. It's also still quite isolating because you don't necessarily have any connection or commonality with the other people in the office.

In short: A good option for those who need a formal office address, meeting rooms and a general professional appearance for their clients.

Don't have a coworking space nearby?

It is possible that a suitable venue isn't nearby, so in this case what do you do? Do you have to give up and retreat back to your home office? Not at all.

Make Jelly: Another option to the fixed, coworking location is the coworking club of no fixed address. Jelly, a group of people who meet at various locations including each other's homes. The facilities might vary; you might end up working on someone's bean bag, but at least you have somewhere to go to and somewhere to get shit done. And if there isn't a Jelly organised near you, you're always able to start one.

Meet up groups: These are springing up all over the place and sites like meetup.com are a good way for you to plug into a professional social circle. They also make it easy to set up if there isn't a professional group near you. The great thing about these is that they are founded on the basis of common interests. It can be as broad as 'self-employed' or as narrow as 'graphic designers'. The down side is that they tend not to meet as frequently as we'd like to foster coworking. Therefore you may want to create your own coworking meet up which gets together twice a week in the mornings for example.

Virtual coworking: For those who are remote or just have difficulty leaving the home another option is online coworking. This isn't a widespread phenomenon amongst solopreneurs but people have been doing a little of it in corporate environments for years. To explain how this works, let me use an example from my time at Microsoft:

Whilst working in England in 2009, we had widespread and heavy snow falls across the country. We couldn't even leave our driveways let alone travel to work. It just wasn't safe. Fortunately though the culture of the organisation let people work from home so we all had the facilities to be online and communicate via instant messaging, web cams and virtual meeting rooms.

For three days, we worked and socialised via the virtual office. We kept all of our meeting schedules. We continued to collaborate on projects and even ask the "hey, what do you think about ..." questions. They just happened through IM instead of being tossed over the partition.

Virtual coworking isn't only for those who can't leave the home or don't have a place to go to. Virtual coworking can also provide valuable tools to help you stay in touch and connected with your coworking space buddies when you're not coworking.

According to Brad Krauskopf, founder of Hub Australia and Third Spaces, virtual coworking is an important supplement to physical coworking: "On any given day more of our Hub network is not at the Hub, than are at the Hub. It's no different to many companies where there are more people out of the office than in it. Maintaining learnings, connections and networks when people aren't in the space is essential to making a coworking community work."

Take, for example, my accountability group. We meet weekly and do a lot at our weekly meeting, but we now have a network of professionals that we can tap on the shoulder on those other four days a week. And we do. Quick questions to the group, "What do you think of ... ?", "Does anyone know anything about ... ?". These quick Q&A sessions are frequently taking place in a closed Facebook group we've set up. With the emergence of smart phones, it's even easier and quicker to send a question or post a tip in real time.

Choosing a coworking solution

Clearly, we'd like to have everything, right? The cool workplace with great facilities, within walking distance and available for the price of a coffee. But now returning to the real world of trade-offs, it's a question of what do we need, what can our business afford and what's available.

Let's assume that all options are available in your town. What will you choose then? As we've seen, there are a lot of options to help you find a third place to work. Your choice of coworking solution will depend on your answers to the following:

1. If you had to travel to co-work, how long would be acceptable?
2. If you had to spend money on coworking, how much could your business afford?
3. How much of your work requires privacy and quiet?
4. How important is it to have a dedicated workspace?
5. Do you need to be able to leave things at the office?
6. Are you looking for vibe or down the line productivity?

The answer to these questions will determine which type of coworking space you need. The good news is that there are a lot to choose from. You can even mix and match.

The important thing is to work out what you need and just start. In doing so, you'll immediately solve a big problem of the home office: you'll have a place to go to and a place to get shit done. There's still more to fix, but this is the first step. The location is the catalyst for the other features we need to introduce: the water cooler, the team and the manager.

Other ways to benefit from your coworking space: Impress your clients

In the past, if you were meeting a client it would usually be in a coffee shop or at their office because you were hardly about to take to them to your home office. Imagine though what it would be like if you brought them into a dynamic environment filled with other people doing great things. Imagine the impact that has on your personal brand and that of your business.

'Success breeds success,' as the saying goes and walking through a coworking foyer and into a glass walled meeting room has the ability to set the right tone for your next meeting. It says to your client that you're living the dream and enjoying a work style that they probably aspire to.

Tips for being a successful co-worker from
Brad Krauskopf, founder of Hub Australia:

1. *You'll get what you give. The first thing you should be doing is going there and sharing learnings and giving to the community.*
2. *You've got to use the coworking space for how you feel that particular day. A well set up coworking space will have a diversity of different spaces for you to work from.*
3. *Get a feel for how the coworking space works, otherwise you'll be 'that annoying guy'.*
4. *Pick the right coworking space for you. Depending on the sort of person you are or the project you're working on, different spaces and communities will suit you better than others.*
5. *Get to know the host. The hosts and curators of a well-run coworking space are going to be your keys to unlocking the value of the community.*

Are you a member of the revolution?

This step in the coworking blueprint is about finding a regular and convenient outlet for productive work. You'll know that you've been successful and tapped into the benefits of coworking when:

1. *You have a regular time and schedule of when you go to your new workplace.*
2. *Your daily productivity increases.*
3. *You look forward to 'going to work'.*
4. *You longer have trouble 'leaving work' at the end of the day.*
5. *You no longer feel isolated in your home office.*

Key points

1. Coworking spaces come in a variety of shapes. There is a trade-off between what you're prepared to pay vs. the facilities you'll receive but spending more isn't necessarily better.
2. The coworking revolution blueprint is about supplementing your home office rather than replacing it. It's also about the people and what you do together, rather than the physical space itself.
3. The important thing is to start. Try a few and get a feel for the space and community there.

Memory bytes

- A place to go is a good 'headspace' tool.
- It helps you be more productive.
- It sets the mood.
- Your options include the local library, cafe, coworking cafes, coworking centres and serviced offices.
- Cheaper options include Jelly, meet up groups and virtual coworking.
- Decide your absolute must-haves and then work out a budget.
- The location is the catalyst for the water cooler, the team and the manager.

CHAPTER 11

This Water Cooler Serves Coffee: Spending Time with the Right People

2nd Inhibitor to home-work success: not working with the right people

- Spending too much time alone in the home office.
- Not seeking out the input and ideas of others.
- Not having a professional social outlet.
- Not having a group to share your wins and knock with.

Coworking blueprint:

Step 1: Find your coworking space.
Step 2: Plug into your community.
Step 3: Build a team.
Step 4: Create an advisory board.

For some reason, when we first thought of going out on our own, we didn't realise we'd actually be *on* our own. Professional isolation and not spending time with the right people is a big inhibitor of success in the home office. To a large extent, it's responsible for our tendency to procrastinate and makes it difficult to get motivated each day.

As we discussed in chapter 5, there are five different social needs we need to fill to keep work fun, stay motivated and keep our sanity:
1. Professional social interaction
2. Professional connection & creativity
3. Serendipitous conversations
4. Social celebrations & rituals.
5. Support and encouragement.

Traditionally, we attempt to meet these needs by attending events such as networking groups, seminars and conferences. On a day-to-day basis, we may go to a local cafe or meet friends for lunch. Then there are those who save it all up for when their partner comes home, and talk their ear off all night. But do any of these things actually fulfil our need for socialisation? Not really.

To address the issue, we need to come up with a solution where interactions are ad hoc and day-to-day which is how serendipity and creativity occur. We also need interaction with other professionals who can relate to our challenges rather than our friends who we talk about the kids with. Catching up with friends over lunch isn't the same. We need a professional circle who is around during 'office hours' to share, support and celebrate with.

How we can use coworking to solve this

Coworking offers the opportunity to solve a lot of these issues through the mere fact that you are working alongside like-minded people on a day-to-day basis. It provides the opportunity to supplement your home office environment with a more social and collaborative environment and replaces those interactions that the traditional office has, but we've left behind.

Professional social interaction

Imagine you're working at home, but you need a change of pace or scene. You go to your favourite coworking space where you find the same dozen or so people who also work for themselves and who share your professional challenges. These are the people you can discuss work with.

107

They may not know anything about your family life and probably won't be talking about what your kids are up to. However they know about what it means to be self-employed and they too are there to work in a social and collaborative environment.

Professional connection and creativity

Now that you've gone to work in your coworking space, you have other people to bounce ideas off. Over coffee you say, "hey what do you think about … " and you'll get a load of great feedback. You no longer need to go crazy bouncing ideas off the guy in the mirror. You also have that synergistic effect where your idea grows from theirs; and back again and so on, until your idea arrives at a new and amazing place.

Serendipitous conversations

We've all gotten to where we are today through at least a small element of chance, but for this to happen we need to be out in the world and fishing in the right pond. Our coworking space is that pond. Here, through ad hoc professional interaction, we're able to leave the door open for the right things to happen, for the right conversations to take place and the right introductions to be made. This just isn't possible from the home office and it's less likely to occur if you're primary social interaction is the monthly chamber of commerce meeting.

Social celebrations and rituals

It's a lot easier to celebrate Melbourne Cup with co-workers when you have them. By their nature, the other people who are at a coworking space also have the same interest in getting out of the house and being more social. So you have a community of like-minded people to share these things with.

Many coworking spaces provide opportunities to celebrate such as Friday afternoon drinks, Melbourne Cup, end of financial year and holiday celebrations. You could even take your own birthday cake along. I'm sure no one is going to mind if you turn up with a triple chocolate mud cake.

Coworking in action

I like to start my week at a coworking cafe and spend an hour or so with people talking through what happened last week and what we hope to achieve this week. It started out as an accountability session, but it quickly evolved into a general exchange of ideas, advice and professional social interaction. For all of us, the week now starts with the fresh creative input of other people who have an idea, know someone or have dealt with the same challenges we're now facing.

In most cases, these conversations just evolve. No one turned up to specifically ask advice. Often we'll end up discussing something that was bubbling around in our subconscious but hadn't brought to the surface until we started to talk about it.

Without a dose of regular, unstructured interaction we miss these opportunities. We dive straight into work without leaving the door open for creativity, serendipity and the fortuitous nudge in the right direction.

Traps and pitfalls

You can socialise but you still need to get the work done

You can always have too much of a good thing and the trap with giving people a social outlet is that they use it as a crutch or an excuse not to get on with the job at hand. We see this in home offices today where some people will spend far too much time on Facebook being social. They might rationalise this by saying they are engaging in social marketing, but often they're just procrastinating because the things they need to get done are too hard or confronting.

Coworking is a great way to get out and work with a more professional circle, but you still need to get the work done. It's fine to take advantage of the social element; this is important. But don't use it as an extended lunchroom. People are also there to work and you need to go there to work too.

Finding your kind of people

Not every coworking space attracts the same type of people so you need to find one that attracts your type of people. For example, some spaces will have a concentration of artists and creatives. This is great if you're a designer but if you're a strategy consultant, you're not going to have much in common. As a result you're not going to find people who relate to your business challenges and it's going to be harder to bounce ideas off one another.

Finding a place that's not all about work

There are also some coworking spaces where people don't interact. Sometimes this is because the layout isn't conducive. Serviced offices have this problem. Sometimes, it's just the social norm that exists.

I once visited a coworking space recommended by a friend who talked about how interesting the owners were; the funky place they'd chosen in the loft of a building and the eclectic mix of furniture and colours on the walls. I was really looking forward to seeing it. What I found though was a very quiet and subdued environment. The space had all of those features, but it was too quiet for me. People weren't interacting and everyone was whispering. This might be fine when you want to get work done but it doesn't help you replace the water cooler, which is what this chapter is about. Remember: *It's not about the space; it's about the people and what you do together.*

Beer on Tap

One of the things I appreciate in my coworking cafe are those who have beer on tap. This is not to say I drink during the day (though I'm sure we all feel that way sometimes) but it definitely sets the tone for my work environment. It signals that this is a fun and interesting place that in turn attracts fun and interesting people. The owners put on Friday drinks every fortnight and this also helps bring the community together.

It needs to be near

Another trap people will fall into is joining a space which is right for all of the right reasons but it's a 20 minute commute to get there. Now if you're using it as a substitute for your home office that might be fine, but we're talking about coworking as a supplement to your home office. If we want it to be our place for ad hoc social interaction, then it needs to be convenient enough to drop into on a whim.

If your coworking space is too far away, you're going to make sure you go there and get work done. As a result you'll probably miss the social, creative and serendipitous opportunities that would otherwise exist.

When coworking feels like you're working at a library

Not all coworking spaces will be the dynamic, hip, fun places you hope they'll be which seems odd when you consider that people have come there to be in a more collaborate workspace. Peta Ellis of River City Labs says that the personalities you have in the room can have a big impact.

"You really notice it when a big personality leaves the space" she says. They seem to be a critical part of the culture or vibe and set the tone for what's happening. So what do you do if you're coworking space is turning into the local library? Well you have two options, you can either be the change you wish to see in the world or you can take yourself off to another space.

It's a hard balance to find, that of getting work done vs. being social. Drawing on the corporate experience again, it often takes someone in a group leadership role to set the tone and a few social occasions to bring people together.

You also need to break the ice. There's no getting away from actually meeting people and knowing them well enough to say hello and ask for help. It's important to get out there and meet your fellow co-workers, find out who they are and what you can do together.

Curated coworking spaces

Adam Kallish believes that vetting independent workers with an eye to creating a collaborative culture where a diversity of skills could establish new alliances adds new value to the coworking concept.

"One of the key challenges of independent workers is a lack of community and camaraderie that was often found at full-time organizations. Humans are social creatures and a lack of daily contact with people like yourself can lead to stress and alienation. At a recent Chicago Humanities Festival discussion on the future of books, Anthony Grafton discussed the historical dissemination of knowledge in coffee shops and other public spaces. He called these areas 'trading zones' that brought people together to create new languages and experiences through the contact of a diversity of people.

The trend of curated coworking is a natural next step in workspaces by emphasizing chemistry and experience trading zones. These environments work as an incubator for independent workers to interact and find new value through discussions and collaborations. Benjamin Dyett, a co-founder of Grind, a New York City curated work environment and the company's chief gatekeeper stated that curated coworking is not to be ... "elitist and exclusive," but rather "It is to create a strong, cohesive community."[5]

What are the coworking options and choosing one that's right

Earlier in the book we've discussed the pros and cons of different coworking solutions. So how do they stack up as a replacement for the office lunchroom? The criteria for replacing the water cooler is that it needs to tick the following boxes:

- ☐ Is it convenient enough to drop into?
- ☐ Is it priced to encourage you to drop in on a whim?
- ☐ Does it foster ad hoc interaction or is it scheduled?
- ☐ Is it a regular day-to-day interaction, sporadic or irregular?
- ☐ Does it foster professional interaction or social interaction?
- ☐ Do you have common professional interests with the people there?
- ☐ Is it a social environment or strictly work?

Serviced Offices: Fine for the professional address, but not a great place to meet and interact with people. The challenge is that you're locked away

---

5   http://www.tropecollaborative.com/blog/2012/04/curated-coworking-environments-the-next-level/

behind the walls of your office so you're not even within earshot of anyone else. You'd get more interaction back at home, talking to the dog again.

Coworking Centres: Some are great for social interaction and all of the things we need to replace the water cooler. Before choosing a coworking centre check out their event calendar to get a feel for how they help their members socialise. Also, drop in at morning tea and lunch to see how people are socialising. Is it an inherently social place or are people just there to work and then leave.

Coworking cafes: Your day-to-day social options here are probably better because the people who have chosen this option are signing up to a more public and social environment by definition.

Cafes, Libraries and Museums: There may be other people here but perhaps not that many working so your socialisation isn't going to be of the professional kind. Opportunities to bump into one another for a chat are going to be a little harder.

Profiting from social coworking

Ok, so you're now a regular feature at your coworking space and enjoying co-worker's birthday cakes every other week, but how does this help your business grow? A large part of the answer is that it's become your new networking outlet.

We've all attended networking functions in the hope that we'd get referrals and eventual business. Now that we have a coworking space where we meet new people regularly, we have a more consistent and genuine network of people who are introduced to our business. Because our interactions are now more genuine and consistent, these are more likely to be based on respect and trust which is how many Asian cultures have been doing business for a long time.

⚬ ⚬ ⚬ ⚬ ⚬ ⚬ ⚬ ⚬ ⚬ ⚬ ⚬

Networking Tip #1:

May King runs a large online business community that also gets together for a monthly networking event. I asked her opinion of the best way to network and she said that the tendency for some people was to stand-up and ask for business right there and then. In her opinion, networking needed to more Chinese in nature where it was still based on the relationship first. In Chinese business culture, people don't try to close the deal at the first meeting. They may not even ask for the business at the second meeting. Instead, they establish whether or not they want to do business together and then they ask for the order.

People do business with those they like, so when you meet someone, put yourself forward, not your business card.

Networking Tip #2: Get your pitch right.

The adage is that you get what you pitch for but so many people when asked what they do, waffle on leaving the listener unclear as to what they do. Even if someone liked you and wanted to do business or refer you to a friend, how could they if they didn't really understand what you do, who you do it for and why you're different?

There are a number of ways to structure a pitch but the best ones are accurate, have an emotive connection with the listener and a memorable fact. We have a number of pitching resources on the Coworking Revolution website if you need a little help putting your pitch together.

The second way in which you're going to profit from being more social is through chance, serendipity or just dumb luck. Now of course we don't want to base our business strategy on being in the right place at the right time, but as we discussed earlier, we've all benefited from the chance encounter that opened a door, introduced us to a client or presented a new opportunity. This isn't happening from your spare room HQ. By getting out, being with people and talking business, you'll find a host of new ideas, opportunities and introductions. Being social is good for business.

Tips for social coworking

Like all group environments, there are social norms that help us fit in. Here are a couple of golden rules to make sure you're doing things right:

1. Be social, but be respectful of those trying to get things done.
2. Limit your socialising to communal spaces and times e.g.: the kitchen at morning tea.
3. Participate. Take along a birthday cake; schedule Friday drinks into your calendar.
4. Take a genuine interest in others and look for ways to help and refer business.

"You'll get what you give. The first thing you should be doing is going there and sharing learnings and giving to the community."
Brad Krauskopf, founder of Hub Australia.

The social advantage of coworking

The bottom line is that working from home can be demotivating and isolating. Coworking gives us a quick fix for this, providing a social outlet in our workday that not only lifts our spirits but connects us with others for inspiration, support and motivation.

The daily struggle to stay motivated is one that many face but it needn't be the case. Find your local, schedule it into a regular part of your daily rhythm and get out of your pyjamas and be social.

Home-Work Motivation Tip: Go with the Flow

Flow is a state of mind first described by noted psychiatrist and author Mihály Csíkszentmihályi. It describes that state of mind we enter when we're totally absorbed by what we're doing. It's characterised by a sense of time flying by and at the end of it, we feel a sense of achievement and satisfaction.

Examples of those in a state of flow are professional sports people, musicians when performing and artists when painting. In each of these examples, the 'artist' is completely absorbed in the moment, they lose all sense of time and are completely engaged in using their skills and abilities. At the end of the 'performance' they experience a sense of joy and satisfaction.

Flow doesn't only apply to elite sports people or artists. Everyone has their own state of flow – even young children. The level of skill and performance applied is different but the state of mind and satisfaction in the end is still the same.

Martin Seligman in his book Authentic Happiness suggests that one way to increase our happiness at work is to understand the activities that create a state of flow for us and to build those into our schedule for the day.

For example, my state of flow comes from activities as diverse as brainstorming and envisioning on one hand and creating financial models in a spreadsheet on the other. I also enter a state of flow when sailing and playing music.

What generates flow is individual to everyone but we all have activities that put us in that space. Knowing this, you can create a little extra emotional support in the home office by scheduling your own flow state activities in your day. Perhaps scheduling these for the end of the day will help you finish on a high and with renewed enthusiasm for what you have to do tomorrow.

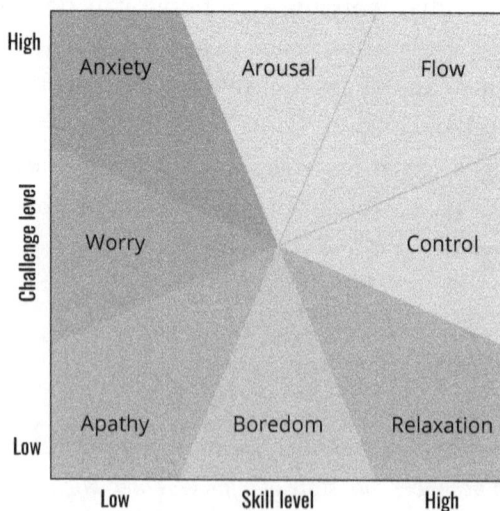

Csikszentmihalyi, M., Finding Flow, 1997

Are you a member of the revolution?

This phase of the blueprint is designed to recreate the water cooler and fulfil the social needs we all have day-to-day. You'll know you've successfully implemented this step when:

1. *You no longer feel isolated working for yourself.*
2. *You have other professionals you socialise with during the week*
3. *You're in a group of people who provide mutual support and encouragement.*

Having implemented the first two phases successfully, you've now addressed the FUNdamentals of the home enterprise. You're now working in the right places, spending time with the right people and as a result, work is a lot more fun and productive.

Key points

1. One of the major inhibitors to success is spending too much time on our own and not spending enough time with the right people.
2. Coworking is an easy way to fix the challenge of professional isolation.
3. By working near others, you're more likely to be self-motivated and productive while you're there.
4. Different coworking options provide different opportunities for social interaction and encourage different communities of people.
5. Once there, be respectful of when to socialise and when to work. People still need to get things done.

Memory bytes

○ Going out on your own doesn't have to mean on your own.
○ Serendipitous conversations through professional social interaction are often a key thought-starter.
○ Choose a space with the people and interaction style you need.
○ Curated coworking is a form of vetting your fellow travellers before engaging a space.
○ The 'water cooler' should be convenient, budget-friendly and fostering of ad hoc professional conversation.
○ Referrals and networking opportunities are more likely from people who know and like us.
○ Being out and about creates the luck business sometimes needs.

To do

Getting started isn't difficult. Just begin by visiting a few different spaces and options that suit you, your budget and location. Here's a quick step-by-step list for those who need a little push out the door:

1. Google 'coworking and shared office space, [your suburb]' and make a list.
2. Schedule two lunch hours this week to visit the coworking spaces you've found. Call to let them know you'll be dropping in so they can show you around.
3. Check the coworking spaces against our social coworking checklist.
4. Try before you buy: Start by scheduling a slot twice a week where you'll visit your coworking space. Make sure you're there across a time when people will be taking a break.
5. After a couple of weeks, revisit the checklist and see if this is your place or if you'd like to try another.

CHAPTER 12

Plugging Back into a Team:
Synergy for the Soloist

syn·er·gy (sĭn'ər-jē)

1. The interaction of two or more agents or forces so that their combined effect is greater than the sum of their individual effects.
2. Cooperative interaction among groups, especially among the acquired subsidiaries or merged parts of a corporation, that creates an enhanced combined effect.

3rd Inhibitor to home-work success: Doing everything yourself

- Not working to your strengths.
- Not taking advantage of other specialists.
- Not creating more value and better quality through synergy and teamwork.

Coworking blueprint:

Step 1: Find your coworking space
Step 2: Plug into your community
Step 3: Build a team
Step 4: Create an advisory board

There's no synergy in a team of one so how do we create synergy for the soloist? As we discussed in chapter 6, there are three advantages the corporate office has over the home office:

1. A pool of expertise allowing things to get done more efficiently.
2. Collaboration between peers delivering better quality, innovation and value to customers.
3. Momentum in the business so that it doesn't rely on the presence of just one person.

We lost the teamwork that comes from a group of people who help us get things done faster and more efficiently. We lost our collaborators, the people who inject new ideas, help us deliver quality products or services and we lost the machine of commerce that keeps turning even when we're not there.

Instead, as a soloist we have to be the jack-of-all-trades, spending more time and money than necessary on tasks. We don't have the synergistic effect of others helping us inject new ideas and value to our customers. And when we're not at work, the whole machine stops.

According to Brad Krauskopf, collaboration has become increasingly important part of the coworking scene. "It's not sufficient for any one person to be brilliant. You need multiple people to be collaborating to produce a solution that's going to be the winning business or idea."

How most people solve this problem traditionally

Pool of expertise vs. Jack-of-all-trades

For homepreneurs, the current solutions to these problems are a little clunky and far from perfect. If we need expertise to help us with our marketing strategy, manage an event or do the accounts, we often just bumble along ourselves, irrespective of how much time we lose in the process. In fact generally, we don't even understand what a solution could look like because we don't know what we don't know. As a result our offering looks clunky and amateurish.

For those who do call upon the expertise of others, this isn't always a simple matter either. Often we need a pointer in the right direction or a little expertise for an hour or so, but how and where do you find this? Assuming you know someone who has the expertise, when are they able to do it? They have their own business to run of course

Collaborators

As soloists, we miss the ability to bounce ideas off people and having others check the quality (and sanity) of our work. We're also limited in the amount of work we can take on or the size of the job because it's not a team that's delivering. It's just you.

At best, soloists may have a buddy they share their ideas with, someone they might send an important report over to or someone they occasionally refer some work to when a bigger job comes along. However, again, the access to quality input isn't always convenient or readily available and this hampers our ability to make this a regular part of the way we work.

Momentum of the business

Whether it's a vacation or a day off sick or just an all-consuming project you're delivering, when you stop working, everything else stops too because ... there's just no one else keeping things running. How do people try to address this currently? Not well.

For short periods, people generally make do. They work longer and later hours and weekends and regretfully, cut a few corners.

For longer absences, work typically just gets deferred. Clients are turned away or scheduled for later in the year. My training friends for example, stop working during their family vacation but this isn't ideal because they have to break the inertia and get things up and rolling again when they're back.

How we can use coworking to solve this

In a coworking environment, our day-to-day professional interaction helps plug us back into a team and by doing so, helps us meet our daily business requirements more efficiently. It gives us better and more readily available access to people we can collaborate with which in turn helps us create a business ecosystem that can maintain a little momentum when we're not on deck.

A pool of expertise, creating efficiency.

In a coworking environment, your co-workers are running all types of businesses and generally have broad expertise in a wide range of business topics. If you need help managing an event, there's probably an event manager in the group. If you need a pointer on which CRM system to use, there'll be someone there who has recently asked the same question. Maybe you just need an hour of help with the SEO on your webpage. There'll probably be a web developer you can lean on.

Even if your immediate group of co-workers don't have that expertise, they have their own network of contacts and can probably put you in contact with the right person.

The advantage of using coworking in this way isn't only that you can find the answers or the expertise faster, but unless it's a substantive job you need done, you'll probably also find the help you need for free. Amongst coworking colleagues, we're always contributing advice and assistance to each other's business. It's nothing for me to give an hour of my time if I can help someone with a quick fix that gets them underway again. Little pointers like this can save people weeks of deliberation.

Coworking gives you access to the pool of expertise that every organisation has but the soloist doesn't.

Collaboration of peers delivering value to customers

Coworking also makes it easier for us to bounce ideas off people and check the quality our work because we have a team on tap. Particularly if they're people we regularly partner with to deliver work.

Collaboration in a coworking environment takes place all the time. Occasionally it might be formal such as asking someone to review a brochure, report or website. More often it's informal and occurs when you're sharing a challenge or an idea over coffee.

Karen, one of the ladies I co-work with, wanted to run a coaching workshop but was new to running events and marketing them. With a little advice from myself and another co-worker, she selected a great venue, created a flyer, wrote her copy and settled on a price all within a week. For us, it was an easy 30 minute conversation over coffee but for Karen it literally saved her weeks of working through these details herself and she might not have had the same quality output as a result.

Creating momentum in the business

Coworking helps us address the momentum issue by having a team of people who can help us backfill our skill requirements when we need to. Need someone to hold the fort whilst you're on holidays? Chances are you know someone who can do this and who probably needs the same from you at some point during the year.

Because you're now part of an informal team of professionals, things can continue to run at least a little longer than they otherwise would.

Coworking in action - The coworking blueprint for teamwork:

Fellow travellers + Collaborative Rhythm + Formalised agreements + Shared commercial dependencies + Options for review and exit = success.

Fellow travellers

The first requirement to unlocking the potential teamwork inherent in a coworking environment is to identify your fellow travellers. Those people who have complementary skills and businesses who you have a mutual respect for and who can benefit from a collaborative working relationship. These people will become your vTeam (virtual team), a term commonly used at Microsoft to describe a cross functional group who would come together regularly to work on a specific project or goal.

For example, with my business mentoring work, my coworking vTeam consists of David, a PR and email marketing specialist, Kathryn a graphic designer, Derek, an accountant and tax specialist, Katey, a social marketing queen and Mark a technology innovator.

What about competing with one another?

This is a common issue for people and particularly so if their business is in the early start-up stages. The thing to remember though is that unless you're working with another person who is running a local flower delivery service (for example), the market is always going to be bigger than you can service alone. Competitive threats from your coworking colleagues are generally more perceived than real. If you're collaborating, then the goal is to grow the size of the pie together, not find ways to take a bigger slice.

Identify and play to your (and others) strengths

One of the really smart ways in which to build a team around you is to understand where your strengths lay and where your blind spots are, not just in terms of skills but also in terms of work styles, and psychological characteristics. Large organisations undertake individual and team based psychological profiling and you may be familiar with tools such as Myers

Briggs or the Herman Brain Dominance Model. I have two favourites that I've always used in organisations, which apply equally well to the soloist and their new coworking vTeam.

Tools for Team Building

Strengths finder: This tool developed by noted psychiatrist Robert Seligman, is based on the premise of understanding what your natural strengths are and playing to those. There's a great online tool that identifies your top five strengths and gives you advice on how to capitalise on those.

Understanding your strengths and playing to them is essential to the soloist as a person who tends to be the jack-of-all-trades. This will shine a light on what to do for ourselves, what to ask for help with and what to look for in others.

Belbin: My other standard tool in the kit bag for building great teams is Dr Meredith Belbin's Team Profiler. This tool is based on the notion that when put into a team, we all tend to default to a role that plays to our strengths and natural style. Again, there's an easy online tool to support your vTeam in doing this. As a result you'll be able to understand how your vTeam best functions together and how to make best use of everyone's natural talents in keeping the team functioning well.

There are links to both of these tools on the Coworking Revolution website: www.risingtideventures.com.au/coworking-revolution.

Team building

The concept of team building doesn't require explanation, but there are obvious reasons why you, the dog and Bruce the ficus aren't going on weekend retreats together. Interestingly, there's not a lot of team building that goes on in a coworking environment either. This isn't to say that it's not important. On the contrary, it's probably more important because your vTeam is, at least in the beginning, going to be a loose collaboration of individuals. A little team building activity for you is still valid and going to be a lot of fun at the same time. It doesn't have to be a week long retreat climbing Mt Kilimanjaro together, but Friday afternoon drinks doesn't count either.

Put it to the group and organise a couple of fun activities that require a little interdependence. For example, Mark invited his vTeam to a one-day seminar together. It was a great way for everyone to learn, share new ideas and spend a little social time together at the end of the day. I like to take my vTeam sailing. This is a great way to take a break from work and requires a little teamwork for us all to get home.

Learning from one another

One of the great things about coworking is your ability to learn from one another, not just in terms of day-to-day advice but also through more structured learning opportunities. Many coworking spaces host events on different topics that are a great way to stay in touch with various business topics and develop your knowledge.

One of the things we like to do is encourage 'Idea Exchanges' where someone with expertise in an area agrees to host a discussion over coffee for anyone interested. For example, Derek is an accountant and hosts discussions on common questions like 'which type of company structure do you need?' These tend to be short, small group discussions rather than formal workshops per se and are a great way for Derek to share information. He also receives a lot of feedback on what people are looking for, what their concerns are and how best to help his clientele. Of course it's also a great way for Derek to position himself as a leader in his field.

Collaborative rhythm

Having identified your fellow travellers, the next requirement is to have a regular rhythm for catching up. This isn't necessarily a formal meeting, but could be as simple as a regular lunch appointment or time slot when you're coworking together.

My collaborative rhythm consists of meeting with my accountability group on a Monday morning, a regular coworking period on a Wednesday morning and a more formal recurring project meeting on Friday mornings. Each takes on a different format but the consistency is what's important.

You can't collaborate effectively if it's sporadic. It also helps to have a formal collaboration meeting to help make the conversation more purposeful. This doesn't mean you have to work closely all the time. It's ok to be just present and available too, but you need a balance of formats and should not just rely on the social, casual interaction.

Formalised agreements

Once you've identified your fellow travellers and have set up a schedule for getting together, it's a good idea to formalise things a little. By formalising, I mean start with documenting the purpose of why you're getting together in the first place, what you hope to achieve out of the collaboration.

Once you start partnering on specific projects or ideas, it's probably time to enter into a formal collaboration agreement and this is better done sooner rather than later. In fact, I like to share a draft of what it would look like long before I start partnering just to set the expectation early and to give people time to review and contribute their own ideas. People tend to have loads of good will during the honeymoon phase so that's the time to share it with everyone. There's an example collaboration agreement on www.risingtideventures.com.au/coworking-revolution.

Shared commercial dependencies

Having collaborated on ideas, advice and the occasional project, you can really ramp up the benefits of coworking teamwork, by starting to explore partnerships or joint ventures in some areas. Some ideas (in order of commitment and complexity):

- Forming a buying group for blogging and copywriting services.
- Sharing the services of a Virtual Assistant or outsourced supplier.
- Formally exchanging a regular amount of time or value with one another (e.g.: one hour per week of marketing in exchange for one hour per week of bookkeeping).
- Contributing and withdrawing from a coworking time bank.
- Running joint events.

- Developing a joint marketing plan to promote complementary services at the same time.
- Sharing distribution of each other's newsletters and content.
- Attending joint sales calls together.
- Joint business planning.
- Joint bidding for a bigger client or project.
- Formalising a referral system and compensation.

A big advantage of developing share dependencies with your vTeam is that this is where the momentum comes from and how it's maintained if you need to step off deck for a short period. This is a big advantage of the traditional organisation and how we as soloists can keep the machine running for a time without us.

Health practitioners have been using locums for ages to cover for them when they're away, keeping the doors open and the patients well. Why don't we use locums in business? It's the same principle and can often work on an exchange basis. For example Chrissy and Michael run a small IT business supporting the professional services industry. They partner with a similar sized IT business on the other side of town so they can still take a family vacation each year. The business stays open; the revenue keeps flowing and the customers are happy. Everyone wins.

Opportunities to review and exit

Like death and taxes, all collaborations, joint ventures or partnerships will end at some point in the future. It's inevitable so the best time to plan for them is early whilst everyone is in the honeymoon phase and their goodwill is at its highest.

A good way to start in the early days is to make the catch up rhythm applicable for a specific period such as eight weeks. That gives everyone the opportunity to see if the dynamic is working for them and if they're getting value out of the process. At the end of eight weeks, people can leave the group or agree to continue.

Set a regular review point to make sure everyone is getting what they want out of it and revisit the objectives for getting together in the first place. These review points are a great, non-confrontational way of allowing people to suggest a course correction or bow out gracefully.

If your collaboration is more substantive and you have shared commercial dependencies, these should be supported with exit clauses that help facilitate a graceful parting of ways. This often happens when someone's business has taken off in a new direction or their needs have changed, but can also occur through conflict. Recognising that all partnerships have a natural life helps you plan for this, part ways gracefully and maintain a good working relationship into the future.

Facilitating your coworking team

As we all know, not much happens without someone pulling it together. Professional organisations, volunteer groups, the local parents and citizens committee, it's all the same. Someone needs to stand at the front and take on the responsibility for organising things. So too with your coworking vTeam.

All of these great ideas, advisory groups, accountability teams, joint business planning and review, even the social functions still need an organiser to make it come together so who will do it? In joining or creating a vTeam, make sure you have someone willing to take on that role, or at least to get the ball rolling. You can of course share the responsibility and you should, but it's going to need a shaper to kick it off in the first instance.

If that's not you, if you're more a contributor than a leader, that's fine. Just put the requirement out to the coworking group and ask someone to put their hand up. One thing that's certain about self-employed people is that they're generally 'the go out and make it happen' types. There's going to be some who will be willing and able to provide that group leadership and facilitation you need.

Traps and pitfalls

Of course we're all human beings and no one is infallible so when you start collaborating with your vTeam keep your feet on the ground and the following tips in mind:

1. Remember it's just the advice of one person. If it's an important decision, hire a professional.
2. Don't be a leech and take without giving. The best policy is to pay it forward.

3. Make sure there's an element of trust with whom you partner with and have a partnering agreement to protect both of your interests. Nothing says I love you like a contract. (See the Coworking Revolution website for a boilerplate template if you need one: www.risingtideventures.com.au/coworking-revolution)

4. Clear up any competitive or conflict of interest issues quickly and refer back to your partnership agreement if in doubt.

How your coworking team helps you profit

So ok, you've got your vTeam in place and you're all sitting around on bean bags tossing ideas around and everyone's feeling great. Are you earning more? You will. At the start of the chapter we said we wanted to foster teamwork because we wanted to recreate three things. Creating these three aspects delivers immediate and tangible results for your business:

- A pool of expertise and resources to work more efficiently: This results in our work getting done faster, particularly the things we're developing prior to launch which in turn allow us to generate income sooner. We can also get this input cheaper, saving us money and because we're going to experts first rather than after we've tried and failed, it saves us from spending twice.

- A team of collaborators who can help drive quality, innovation and value for our customers: How much time have we lost on ideas that didn't really take off or how much has it cost you if something's gone to a customer that wasn't quite right? Having people to sanity test our work and bounce ideas off protects our value in the market.

- Momentum in the business so that the wheels keep turning when we're not there: How much work have you had to turn away because you were busy or on vacation? Having someone there to hold the fort might mean you need to share a little profit but at least it's still coming in and your customers are happy.

If you're able to create a more formal alliance and share back office or sales and marketing expenses this is good for business too. Not only will it reduce your cost structure, but having a more comprehensive offering might actually win you more business.

Other ways to benefit from your vTeam

Product advisory group

We all need to sanity check our ideas. A great way to leverage your coworking team is to create a product (or service) advisory group. This is a group that gives you feedback on a proposed product or service, whether it would work for them and most importantly, whether or not they would pay for it.

Of course it only counts if your co-workers are representative of the target market, but they are a handy source of feedback none the less. You see, one of the traps of the entrepreneur is that we see opportunities everywhere, but a good idea over a glass of red, does not a business make. Even if the idea is sound and you have a solution to a problem in the market, the way you communicate your offer, price it and make it available still might be off.

As an example, when we were starting '2nd Base' we got to a point where the doors were open but no one was coming in. We sat there scratching our heads because whenever we met a group of soloists and described what we were building, they understood immediately and loved the idea. So where was everyone?

We pulled together a product advisory group and put the problem to them. They immediately focused in on the website. What we'd done was try some fun, new web technologies in our website. Being from a digital and IT industry, we charged ahead and created a cool navigation structure based on our logo and did some fun things with how the information was displayed. Our advisory group however said it was too hard to understand, too difficult to find things and too wordy.

We went back to the group with two other mock-ups and they were still wrong. Finally, I showed them a link to a competitor's website and said, "Do you mean like this?" And they said yes. At the time I was annoyed that we'd hamstrung our fledgling enterprise over a website design; I could see that what we'd designed was a site that we were used to seeing for technologists, not a site that is more suited to a consumer market.

The good news was that the course correction, the round of feedback, trials and iterations only took three days. It could have been a lot worse. Many businesses would continue to bumble along because they don't have ready access to an advisory group.

The important lesson here is don't market to yourself. Use your co-workers to give you feedback on your pitch, your offer to the market and how it's communicated.

Perfecting your pitch

Another problem that affects most people, soloist or corporate, is that they can't represent what they do accurately. We've all been in a situation where someone asks you to introduce yourself and you bumble through an explanation of your business and offering. We've also all been on the receiving end of these descriptions and at the end of the dissertation been no wiser or just nodded politely and moved on.

Having a great pitch is an important first step in marketing your business and again your co-workers are a great source of feedback for whether you're singing on key.

Your pitch needs to be memorable, needs to be accurate and ideally make the listener empathise with the problem, creating an emotive response. Tips for creating a great pitch are available on www.risingtideventures.com.au/coworking-revolution.

Building a team through virtual coworking

There is more than one way to build a team around you, other than creating one through your co-workers, and this is by hiring one.

The growth in micro consulting, outsourcing and virtual assistance is astonishing and as soloists, we're able to take advantage of this to build a bigger team around us than we could otherwise justify or afford.

Imagine for example, all of the possible roles there are in a business e.g.:

Marketing
- Marketing planning
- Designing
- Copywriting
- Webmaster
- Event management
- PR and publicity
- Advertising

Sales
- Business development (prospecting)
- Account management
    - Appointment setting
    - Client updates
    - Client entertainment
- Negotiation

Product or Service Delivery
- Project management
- Supplier management
- Partner management
- Quality assurance
- Process development and documentation

Finance
- Invoicing
- Accounts receivable
- Financial forecasting
- Accounts payable
- Management reporting

Administration
- Correspondence
- Regulatory compliance
- Insurance
- Record management

How many of these thing are you good at? How many of these things do you want to do? How many are aligned with the way you personally deliver value vs. being a requirement of the business? Which of them do you procrastinate on?

For everything other than your personal core value, there will be someone for whom this is their core value. Wouldn't it be better to outsource this to them?

There are a couple of reasons people don't outsource more. Firstly they don't know where to go, secondly they don't know how to structure and manage it and thirdly, they are concerned about how much it will cost their fledgling business. Well, there are answers for all of these.

The first one is an easy one to solve. You can easily find people to meet your service gaps in places such as oDesk.com, elance.com or even better, your local business community. Putting out a request for assistance through a business related Facebook or meetup.com group will put you in touch with the right people. As too will a search via LinkedIn. Before you know it, you'll have offers from people to do everything but run your business.

The second hurdle, how to manage this work, takes a little more planning but it's not difficult either. To successfully manage your outsourced team you need to:

1. Document the process you want them to follow. Just as if you were onboarding a new employee.
2. Give them a template to use for the outputs, where possible.
3. Specify when the deliverable is due and how often you want them to give you a progress report or to send you the work in progress.
4. Review their work and provide regular feedback.

Start by sending them a sample or trial assignment. This will give you an opportunity to test their skills and also iron out your own process and templates. Once you've completed your trial, you can send across your first package of work and then proceed as and when required.

Platforms like oDesk.com have a great dispute resolution process which helps manage things in the event of a dispute. Ideally though, you'll find someone you can work with locally and who becomes such an interdependent part of your business that disputes are few and far between.

Don't put all of your eggs in one basket.

Businesses know too well that you never want to rely on just one supplier. It creates a dependency in your business that you have little control over and if it goes pear-shaped, can jeopardise your ability to deliver.

A co-worker of mine is in the digital marketing space and worked very closely with a local web developer who did all of his client's websites. Things progressed well in their collaboration and they both were able to deliver great results for the client, until the web developer landed their own large, lucrative contract. All of a sudden, websites weren't being delivered, deadlines were slipping and phone calls weren't being returned. The impact on his business was enormous and the damage to his brand was significant, all because he'd been let down by a key supplier. The lesson he learnt was not to put all of his eggs in one basket and not to pay for services until they'd been delivered. Now with a portfolio of suppliers, he can balance the workload between them and if one goes off the boil he can transfer the work to another without losing cash or face.

The third reason people don't outsource is because of the cash outlay. They would like to build a team of experts around them but are concerned they can't afford it. My answer here is to try a little at a time. Start with an amount you can afford and an area where you really need the help or the headspace and see how it works for you.

For example, you might decide you can afford $30 per fortnight over six weeks, $90 across a month and a half (pretty affordable for most home businesses). Your biggest challenge might be staying on top of your invoicing and time sheets. An ad on oDesk for a virtual assistant to help you with your invoicing will return over 200 results costing you between $5 and $15 per hour so you can buy between two and six hours per fortnight of external help which might look like this:

1. At the end of each week, review my calendar and update client invoices with actual time spent.
2. At the end of each fortnight send an invoice to any customer whose invoice exceeds $500 except for those flagged as monthly invoices.
3. Fortnightly, review outstanding invoices and send a statement to any customer who has not yet paid.
4. Fortnightly, for any customer who is more than 30 days overdue, send an email enquiry regarding payment. Schedule time for a phone call in your diary for anyone who doesn't respond.

If staying on top of your invoicing is a problem, outsourcing a process like this is going to create huge value to your business; not to mention give you the additional headspace to focus on bigger and more important tasks that deliver value or help grow your business.

Tips for managing your outsourcer from oDesk.com's Whitney Priest, manager of Enterprise Services[6]

1. Scan skills and experience for similar projects. If any past oDesk project was a publicly posted job, you can click on the job

---

6   From: 'Rules for Reviewing Freelancer Profiles: Find Your Best Hire!' by Whitney Priest

title in the work history and see the job description. "If you're hiring a php developer," Whitney points out, "and all the jobs listed on the profile are in another programming language, the contractor's work history isn't going to be much help. Look for similar projects."

2. Examine the work history for feedback. Sometimes employers rely too much on test scores and stated skills, overlooking the feedback and references on the actual work history. "Looking at prior work experience and feedback on oDesk is valuable," Whitney advises, "However, if the employee doesn't have a lot of experience on oDesk, I recommend reviewing their resume and asking for references from a previous employer. Whether it's an email address -- a company address not a personal one -- a phone number, or written reference, it's good to at least ask."

3. Watch the feedback and work history for repeat customers. Whitney cautions that while this shouldn't be used to exclude potential hires, having repeat employers is a great indicator that the freelancer meets expectations. Whitney says even if you can't see that an employer has hired the contractor more than once, check their feedback for signs of potential rehires. "Sometimes an employer will say something like, 'I'll definitely use this person in the future,' says Whitney. "Having repeat customers is always a good sign."

4. You have to do MORE than research the profile: interview, interview, interview. "You can't just hire from the profile," says Whitney. "It's important to interview people, just as you would in your office." She is quick to point out how many cues and indicators about a person can reveal themselves in the interview process. "You can gauge a person's communications skills when you start interacting with them," Whitney notes. "And part of the interview process is seeing if the contractor can put the interview on her calendar and call in on time."

Professional time bank

Don't have a dime to spare? Well if you need some help but can't afford to hire it, borrow from a time bank.

Time banking is a concept that started in volunteer communities where someone would contribute an hour of their time into the time bank. That gave them a credit and in return they could use that credit from someone else who participated in the time bank scheme. For example, Mary might be too old to push the mower around but she's still a force to be reckoned with at the church cake stall. Bob is happy to work all day long but can't bake a cake to save his life and wants to do something special for his daughter's birthday. Bob contributes an hour of mowing time; Mary contributes an hour of baking and everyone's happy.

The same concept of course can be used in professional circles. One of the ladies in my accountability group was running a coaching workshop and designing a flyer for it. Another lady wanted to come along and was a desktop publisher. She offered to trade services so they both could win.

Of course it's not always possible to find someone to swap skills with so time banking allows everyone to contribute an hour of their time and to withdraw from anyone else. If you're starting up on the smell of an oily rag and can't afford to build a team around you, time banking might help. Find or create a time bank scheme in your local business community. Even better, create one in your local coworking space.

* *

Home-Work Tip: More sales fixes a lot of problems

The pressure to generate income, find that next client and renew that next contract is a big one. For those in the pre-breakthrough phase, this is a constant struggle to bring in work and it can taint everything we do and every interaction we have. This in turn makes us less likely to succeed because we are going to appear less attractive (more desperate) to the market.

The good news is that most of us do have a good product or service – we are good at what we do. This issue is that we just haven't been able to reach our target market effectively.

There are a lot of ways to market your business and to reach people but one simple step that I'd encourage you to do is to create a sales pipeline. This is a simple format that shows you who you've met, who is a potential customer, who would like to know more and who is getting close to signing, (you'll find a simple template for this on www.risingtideventures.com.au/coworking-revolution).

Fill this out, print it and then stick it on the wall beside your monitor. Your goal is to increase the numbers at the very first level; the people who could be interested in your business, by five people each week. This is easy. Attend a networking event, participate in forums, ask friends or existing customers for referrals, look through LinkedIn. One new person per day that you can contact and put your story in front of.

Stay in touch with your clients and prospects

How much money do you leave on the table by disappearing from view after you've met someone or finished a project with a client? What's the likelihood of doing business with that person again or having them refer you to a friend if you did?

A contact management system is a simple and highly rewarding tool for every business but especially a homepreneur. So what do you do?

Firstly you need all of your prospects, clients and contacts in a database. Many people use LinkedIn but I prefer something like MailChimp that gives you a little more flexibility. You can also use a spreadsheet if you prefer.

Whatever system you use, you need to be able to track a couple of things. Firstly you need to know where you met them, what they do and what you last spoke about. Secondly and most importantly, you need to be able to track when they last heard from you.

Each day, you filter your contact history from oldest to newest and take a look at the five people who you've not said hello to but would like to stay in touch with. For these people, you look for opportunities to send them a quick note with something thoughtful, relevant and of value. For example, if I find an article that I think might relate to them, I forward it on. If I do a search on LinkedIn *and find an update about them or their business, I send a note of congratulations. Even better, if I know of an opportunity I can refer them to or even just someone in their industry that I think they'd enjoy meeting, I offer to put them in touch.*

It's a small gesture, but one that demonstrates the value you place on that professional relationship. 99 per cent of people don't do it, so if you are the 1 per cent who does and you do it consistently, you'll stand out and be top of mind when they need help with something. It's a small habit to start, but takes no longer than tracking your company Facebook page and has a much bigger payoff.

If you don't have a plan to connect three times, save your money

In designing a marketing campaign, activity or event, many people make the mistake of focusing on the one hit wonder. The big event that they want everyone to come to. The splashy ad to bring them to your Facebook site. The speaking event at your local chamber of commerce. The flaw with this however is that people don't do business with one hit wonders. Sure you might pick up the odd lead or make such an impression that someone comes over and wants to talk to you further, but most people will forget you after that single interaction. You need to have a plan to 'touch' that contact at least three times for them to recall who you are and possibly develop enough regard for you to do business or refer a friend.

What's required then is a little planning in advance. What's your call to action? How do you plan to stay in touch with that audience after you've attended the networking event? Say you're speaking to a group of people, an example of how you might stay in touch would be asking the organisers if they would distribute an article you've written to the audience, the week after you speak. You might also ask if them if you can write an article for their newsletter the following month. Before you know it, you've just reinforced that wonderful first impression you created and given people the chance over time to remember you and work out how they might benefit from staying in touch. Which reminds me, cultivating the ability to stay in touch is key. You don't have to sell your product on the first presentation and probably won't, so make sure you're building your database of people you meet and could use your product or service, even if they don't know it yet. A word of warning though, don't rely on Facebook Likes or LinkedIn connections.

These are ok, but you've effectively lost control of your data and your ability to connect with people. Facebook changes their contact rules all the time. For example, if you post an update on your company page, only a portion of your fans will have that post delivered to them unless you pay for it. Your database is your asset, so make sure you own it.

Some sales happen through good luck, but great salespeople make their own luck and know that it's consistency and discipline that get results. So every day, put aside 30 minutes to interact with others in the world and go out to meet people. Little by little, your pipeline will grow and before too long, you'll see the fruits of your labour.

Are you a member of the revolution?

This step in the coworking blueprint is about taking the foundation of working in the right places, with the right people and then activating the benefits of teamwork and collaboration. It's based on the premise that whilst you might be great at what you do, you can always achieve more as a group.

You'll know that you've been successful and tapped into the benefits of coworking when:

1. *Your work is more creative and you enjoy bouncing ideas off people.*
2. *The skills you have at hand are equivalent to those that exist in a large organisation.*
3. *You have the ability to scale your work. No project is too big or outside your specialty.*
4. *Your business can operate for a time without you. You're no longer concerned about taking vacations.*

Key points

1. The coworking revolution isn't just about the place; it's also about the people and what you do together. If you don't want to be an amateur delivering amateur results, you're going to need others to fill your skill gaps.
2. Your lack of skills and scale are natural inhibitors to the successful and balanced career.
3. Coworking spaces are where you can find and build a vTeam but the style of coworking also allows you to buy in online and remote resources such as virtual assistants and offshore specialists.
4. To make it more than an idea, you have to do business together. This can start with a simple exchange of skills but is even more powerful if you're bidding for work together or referring business to one another.

Memory bytes

- Plug into a network of collaborators who will help in more ways than you know.
- Give and ye shall receive!
- A team gets stuff done quicker and in the best possible way.
- Competitive threats from your coworking colleagues are generally more perceived than real.
- Use team builder tools to create your dream team.
- Hold regular meetings.
- Share formal structures that provide value for all in the group.
- Your team will need a leader – is that you?

- Pay your contribution forward.
- A vTeam can share costs, keep the door open and bring experts into the fold.
- Outsourcing means you get a better job done and don't have to do it all yourself.

To do

1. The first step to collaboration and tapping into a new pool of expertise is to be present and consistent. It's not going to work if you're only seen once a month.
2. Like all business, it starts with relationships so begin with those people you already know.
3. Chances are you'll need to broaden your base so if you're not already, start mixing in the right professional circles such as networking groups, professional meet ups and social functions.
4. Invite them for coffee and suggest a regular catch up to discuss business challenges, exchange ideas or form an accountability group. All groups need a purpose though so make sure you outline what you're trying to achieve and give people the option to buy in or not.
5. Understand each other's strengths and team build.
6. Once you have a track record with people and some have drifted in or out, try formalising your cross referral scheme and playing with ideas on how you might present a joint offering to the market.

CHAPTER 13

Chairman of the Board: Solving the Leadership Gap

4th Inhibitor to home-work success: Lack of leadership

- Heading in the wrong direction.
- Not aiming high enough.
- Not having the perspective, or expertise to make your business as good as it can be.
- Not having the accountability to drive towards a result.

Coworking blueprint:

Step 1: Find your coworking space.
Step 2: Plug into your community.
Step 3: Build a team.
Step 4: Create an advisory board

Earlier in the book we discussed how we might not like the idea of a manager, but there are some aspects of leadership and management that don't exist in the home-based business:

1. Accountability: Someone to drive progress.
2. Professional Development: Someone to provide feedback,

development opportunities and stretch us professionally and inspire us to do better.

3. Leadership: Someone to set the strategy, review the plan, inspire us when it gets tough.

What we need, what we do instead and why:

As much as we might like our independence, it's undeniable that everyone benefits from having a leader and mentor nearby and someone who can take a tough line with us when we need it. Even the captains of industry are still accountable to someone and have mentors nearby.

How people try to solve this traditionally (and why it doesn't work)

Accountability

Most soloists understand the need to get things done and will have a view of their goals for the week, month or longer. Our weakness though is in holding ourselves accountable to delivering against those goals.

Why don't we do it? There are a host of reasons but simply put, it's pretty hard to be objective and to hold yourself to account. No one's giving you a kick up the bum if you don't do something; it's not going to appear on your annual performance review.

The one exception to this is if it's a deliverable for a customer. If there's someone paying an invoice based on your work at the end of the week then that tends to focus your attention. But what about all of the things you need to do to get that customer? It's in the preparation for success that we fall down.

We typically try to solve this by creating lists: To do lists, To not do lists, Got done lists. I even read an article once suggesting you have 60 folders where you stick your future lists of things to get done. Crazy.

Some of the more disciplined of us will have vision boards and a weekly review where we connect with our purpose and set goals for the week. This is not bad; being purposeful and having an aligned plan is definitely a good idea, but if you don't make it that week, what happens? Nothing of course. There's just not a great answer to this.

* *

Home-Work Tip: GOST – Goals, objectives, strategies and tactics.

The idea of a large business running without goals and strategy would be ludicrous. They would be an organisation without purpose. They would drift aimlessly through the market, confuse their customers as to what they were trying to achieve and their competitors would walk all over them. Why would we think then that this wouldn't apply to our own home-based business?

A strategic plan is just as important to the soloist as it is to the multinational and here's why:

Vision and Mission statements: These things get a lot of criticism in large organisations because staff typically have a hard time relating to them. For you however, it's your vision for the business and your mission in life that you're expressing so it's entirely relevant. The time thinking and writing these up will provide that 'North Star' that you aim for and help connect with what you're trying to achieve. This is particularly useful on those days when it can be a little hard to get started or you've had the wind knocked out of your sails. If you understand your 'Why', it's easier to dust yourself off and get back on the horse when you get knocked off.

Goals: Goals then, are just a factual and numerical statement of your vision at certain points in time. For example, my vision for '2nd Base' is a future where all home-based entrepreneurs leave their home office and join their community for a while. My goals then are to have X people, working together at Y locations by the end of the year.

Without documenting your goals it's pretty hard to hold yourself accountable and as many people tell us, those who have written goals are much more likely to achieve them than those who don't.

Strategy: I actually dislike this word because it confuses people and sends them down a hole debating whether something is a strategy or a tactic, which is a pointless debate anyway. Instead, let's call it our road map. The general plan of how you're going to achieve your goals and the sequence of things you need to do along the way to make that happen. If you express this as a picture, even better. It forces you to be sequential and draw lines between the things that have to happen first or in parallel.

Documenting your strategy like this also helps you simplify the plan and give you focus so that when you're planning your week, you can take a look at the current step you're at and do some more work on that one.

Leadership

Some entrepreneurs recognise the need for guidance, stretching and a little direction in their business and engage a professional business mentor or coach to help. This is an excellent solution to some aspects of our missing leadership but unfortunately, it's not accessible to all because, quite rightly, they are an expensive resource and beyond the budget of many home-based businesses. As good as they are, they are also an infrequent resource that doesn't help with some of the day-to-day inspiration we need.

Other ways in which we attempt to fill the leadership gap are through mentoring arrangements. These can take a formal or informal role and if selected wisely, can provide a good source of inspiration and perspective on your business challenges. The downside is that there's no accountability or responsibility here and if your mentor buddy starts playing the heavy with you, you might just as easily ditch them.

Professional development

This tends to not happen or is deprioritised. For me, I love to learn and yet I still didn't do it. Now I take a fresh look at those conference brochures that come across my desk but it's still infrequent and you don't actually retain much of what you heard anyway.

Microsoft take an approach to training which is 10 per cent formal coursework, 20 per cent learning from others and 70 per cent on-the-job training. This on-the-job training happens a lot because we're trying to be jack-of-all-trades, but we're not learning from others.

But this issue isn't just about formal learning. The issue here is who is stretching you out of your comfort zone. Who is telling you when your work is not good enough and demanding better? A good manager sees clearly your current strengths and weaknesses; can see your potential and what you can become and understands what the next steps look like. They are able to give you the formal training, mentoring and experience you need so you can start on that development journey. This just isn't happening on your own and there isn't a ready solution that people have come up with.

How does coworking provide a catalyst to solve this?

Solving the leadership gap isn't so much about the coworking space as it is about the coworking style of working, i.e.: forming a close collaboration of soloists who know, help and support each other.

Accountability

By forming our team of collaborators, we're also able share our goals and create some mutual accountability. For example, through our coworking community I formed an accountability group that meets first thing every Monday morning. At this meeting we 'declare' our goals for the week and some of the specific actions that will help us accomplish those. We also review last week's progress and present this to the group too. A good accountability group gives its members permission to hold each other to account and to call 'bullshit' if we're letting ourselves off the hook or making excuses.

(a copy of our accountability meeting template is available on www. risingtideventures.com.au/coworking-revolution)

Coworking blueprint for leadership and oversight

Honest Feedback x (Accountability Group + Joint Business Planning + Quarterly Review) = Coworking Advisory Board

Management team

This part of our coworking blueprint is for the advanced players in the team. It requires an inner circle of professionals you trust and respect and who are willing to participate in some more formal assessments of you and your business. Doing this will unlock potential that you're unlikely to find on your own.

Accountability group

This is a group that meets weekly to share their objectives for the week and to report back on their progress of the past week. It's a great driver for starting each week with a documented plan and gives you the opportunity to have a public declaration of goals that will help you stay on track. Having to report back on your results the following Monday also helps drive to completion.

The meetings are best face-to-face but are also possible by Skype or conference call. The important ingredients are a regular rhythm, honest feedback (particularly if people continually miss their targets) and a tight agenda so that people can get back to their own work.

It's important to not let people off the hook all the time. Remember, one of the things we miss out on is having regular accountability from a manager and this process is our tool for reinstating this. It won't work if we don't follow through with the hard questions.

You're able to download a template for running your accountability groups on www.risingtideventures.com.au/coworking-revolution.

Joint business planning

So we've agreed that having a business plan is important. You can't develop a great one on your own though. You need the input and perspective of others to make sure it's robust, practical and realistic for the coming year.

Fortunately your coworking management team have the same needs, so it's a great opportunity for you to plan together and get a little inspiration in the process.

Many people have their preferred formats, templates and styles for business planning. The format or methodology you use isn't as important though as the discussion so I'd recommend that once a week over four weeks, your accountability group shifts focus to business planning along the following lines:

Week 1: Vision & Mission.

Week 2: Goals & Objectives.

Week 3: Assess your strengths, weaknesses, opportunities & threats (SWOT).

Week 4: Road map (addressing each element of the SWOT).

The business planning consultant amongst you will be tempted to build this out further and put extra process in place but don't. Our goal here is to coach others through their own thinking. These are topics for discussion rather than workshops where we develop it for a person. The important thing is not the format, the template or the font you might use in your beautifully bound business plan. The important thing is to ask the questions of yourself, get feedback and input from your peers and then document your answers.

Quarterly review

A plan isn't much good if you don't review yourself and your business against it. Like our business planning session, we need to dedicate a couple of our accountability sessions to review to keep us and our business on track.

The easier review session is for that of your business. You've previously set out the goals and objectives for your business so it should be a simple matter to dust that off and bring it along to present to the group. You should report on your progress against targets, things that have gone well, things that haven't and any new opportunities or challenges that will affect your future objectives. You should also forecast, restate or recommit to your objectives for the next quarter.

Your personal review can be a more confronting experience for some, but as my coach used to tell me, feedback is a gift (even if it makes you wince). It's also necessary if we want that element of objectivity on our own performance and development opportunities that we miss out on by not having a manager.

Personally, I want to know if someone sees a blind spot in my personal performance. Similarly, I want to know someone else's opinion of the next area I could work on to become more competent or professional. Feedback like this is a huge gift because without it, we don't progress.

You can download the personal performance review template and the 360 degree review template from www.risingtideventures.com.au/coworking-revolution.

Traps and pitfalls:

- Not being honest enough.
- Not being respectful enough.
- Not meeting regularly for accountabilities sessions.
- Not being reliable in turning up.
- Not preparing for your discussions.
- Not prioritising time for review.
- Not doing any business planning.
- Getting too caught up in the process. The fact that you're even thinking about the topic puts you ahead of the game.
- Not keeping the plan in front of you and revisiting it.

A fun way to articulate your vision and 'Why' is through a vision board. This is a series of images you collect which represent what the future will look like once you've succeeded (as you define it). It can have images of customers, what they're doing, images of your family and what your life is like. Anything that has meaning to you.

My vision board has images of people connecting and working together and having fun in an attractive cafe; I have an image of my wife and I enjoying lunch together and a family image of us living overseas. These are all personal things that keep me focused on what I'm working to achieve and why.

How this helps us profit from coworking

If you fail to plan, then you plan to fail.

Put simply, our new management team helps ensure we understand our direction, are working towards it in meaningful ways and we are developing our own value, competence and professionalism at the same time. As a result, our business develops faster and we develop our own personal value (which many soloists are selling), which has greater value for customers. Put simply, customers will pay more for your expertise and your business will earn more sooner, as it grows and matures.

Without it, you run the risk of being undervalued, under recognised and under paid. Your business runs the risk of stagnating or falling into decline.

How to get started:

1. *Form your accountability group and start meeting using the template available on www.risingtideventures.com.au/coworking-revolution. Build up the rhythm, habit and trust within your group for a couple of months.*
2. *Schedule your business planning series for month three. Each week for four weeks, discuss one of the business planning topics below and write down the outcomes. Help your group be accountable by having to post these up to your group workspace.*
    Week 1: Vision & Mission.
    Week 2: Goals & Objectives.
    Week 3: Assess your strengths, weaknesses, opportunities & threats (SWOT).
    Week 4: Road map (addressing each element of the SWOT)
3. *Schedule your quarterly reviews*
    a. *Dedicate one meeting to reviewing business objectives and one to reviewing personal performance.*

As we said at the start of this chapter, these concepts are more advanced levels of collaboration for coworking; but it's possible to start light and informal and move to more formalised review and accountability sessions if that's yours and the group's preference.

● ●

Home-Work Tip: To earn more money,
find a way to serve more people

I love the book written by Bob Burg, The Go Giver. It's a great little parable about one man's journey to find business success and how through the mentoring of a wise business leader, he discovers it's not about doing deals on Wall St. Instead, it has at its heart a simple premise: Your income is determined by the amount of value you deliver to others and if you want to earn more, find a way to serve more people.

Having worked in the IT industry for 20 years and been a long-time student of business and leadership, I love this philosophy. It encourages service and value first. It emphasises the genuine interaction between people and recognises that you have to create value to receive it.

● ●

Key points

1. No matter how good you are, you simply don't have the perspective that an outsider has, to see what's going on in the business. Everyone needs an advisor and your coworking vTeam is a good source of perspective.
2. Accountability and review are essential in every business. Your coworking vTeam can fill the role of advisory board members for one another.
3. Everyone can benefit from a level of expertise higher than their own abilities. Working with the right mentor or coach will take your business to the next level and this is something you can share with your vTeam.

Memory bytes

○ We need accountability.
○ We need a road map – a set of goals that delivers our vision.
○ A mentor of some sort is a vital tool.
○ Have an accountability group.
○ Systemise the process with business plans and quarterly reporting.
○ A management group helps you plan and achieve your goals.

CHAPTER 14

The Enviable Life of the Latte-preneur

As we've discussed, there are four critical ingredients required if we are to have a successful, energised and balanced home enterprise. We need:

1. A work environment that encourages productivity and professionalism.
2. To spend time with the right people (for our sanity).
3. To build a team around us who can help us deliver, grow and improve.
4. A leadership and accountability influence in our business to drive the direction, progress and results we desire.

The Coworking Revolution is a new strategy and style of working that helps us as build these four missing ingredients into our day-to-day working lives. It allows us to take advantage of professional spaces that supplement the home office, plug back into a professional social circle and gives us access to the expertise, resources and groups that will help us succeed.

We all start our businesses with ambition, passion, excitement and hope. I am genuinely thrilled and emboldened by the courage people take and the passion they tap into when starting their business. It inspires me and others to take that bold step and create something born out of their imagination and desire.

My hope for you is that realise your dream. That your home enterprise blooms and becomes the success you dream of, whether that's realised in financial terms or just the freedom to spend more time with your family.

Take comfort in the fact that you are not alone on the journey. The coworking revolution is here and is a new way for the professional village to come together once again. To help you connect with this new possibility,

I'd like to share with you my vision for success in the hope that you will find some small parallel to your own desires.

I see a future where:

I wake up energised each Monday morning. Excited by the prospect of the exciting things I will do and the wonderful people I'll work with during the week.

My family time in the morning is a happy one because my enthusiasm for life is infectious. I am completely in the moment with my wife and kids. Work and financial pressures no longer distract me from my time with them.

When I do sit down to start the week, it's with my vTeam and we discuss goals and plans for the week. It's a wonderfully social, enlivening time and connects me with my higher purpose and gives me the drive and motivation to get going.

My days evolve during the week in a similar fashion. Sometimes my colleagues and I catch up for an impromptu coffee before getting back to work. Other times, we're discussing a client we're about to jointly pitch our services to. I especially love the client projects we're working on together. Picking up the phone or exchanging the quick text with an idea or having someone to share a problem with is great. I feel I have the best of both worlds. I am master of my own destiny AND I'm able to share it with others.

I especially love the time I'm now able to work on my business, rather than just in it. My review meetings with my vTeam advisors are really valuable and help me to aim higher and stick to my plans and commitments.

My clients are seeing the difference too. Somehow I have a new confidence and swagger to my approach. My clients find my work-life balance enviable and love to hear my stories of the interesting places I'm working and the people I'm working with.

My family are happier too. No more working until 11pm every night. No more sneaking off after dinner, back into the home office. I'm able to leave work again and focus on being a dad and husband.

My finances are freer, my time to relax is greater and we're back to the security and stability we used to have when I was an employee, only this time, I'm creating it for myself rather than someone else.

All in all, my business is more fun, more successful and more balanced than ever before and it's because I now have other offices which let me leave home when I need to and leave work behind at the end of the day. I have workplaces that are free from distraction and allow me to be more productive, freeing up my time to relax and spend with my family in the evening.

I have professional colleagues again. People who recognise me, understand what I'm trying to get done and who can offer an ear and lend an opinion when I need it.

I no longer have to do it all on my own either. I've been able to build a team around me of people I know locally and those I work with online and internationally. Somehow I've become a solopreneur with an entire team of specialists on hand. Together we bid for work, deliver client projects, innovate and explore new opportunities. I love the creative process we're in and the way in which one idea bounces off another. My business is more successful because I'm no longer limited by what I can achieve alone.

And I'm excited by the future. The people who provide guidance and advice have really opened up my eyes to the possibilities around me. My horizons are much wider now and the things I'm working on will take me towards bigger goals than ever before.

This is my personal vision for success and hopefully it resonates a little with you too. I believe we're all capable of great things. And with the help and guidance of people around us, we can shape, package and share that special gift with a broader market than before and in such a way that doesn't burn you into the ground in the process.

Sure you need to work hard in business, but I've always held two central beliefs in my career:

1. Instead of working 'hard', work smart.
2. If it's something you're passionate about, it's not hard, it's energising.

There are a lot tips, guidance and suggestions in this book but remember at its core, it's about four simple things: Work in the right places. Spend time with the right people. Build a team around you. Bring on board, brains better than yours.

There are a lot of ways to execute this plan. The coworking revolution is a great one though because it alone provides a single catalyst to unlock these four things and in doing so, your home business will have removed the inhibitors and recreated the four ingredients to success that you left behind when you went out on your own.

ABOUT THE AUTHOR

Matthew Dunstan is an adventurer at heart with a passion for exploring, teaching and mentoring others.

Matthew has been a lecturer of International Marketing at Griffith University. He has also taught Information Technology Management and Process Improvement for the Australian Graduate School of Management's Executive MBA program. Matthew has designed and led major change initiatives for teams of over 100 people and managed organisations responsible for over $300 million in revenue.

In 2010, Matthew Dunstan turned away from a successful career at Microsoft to pursue his dream of sailing the world with his family. After a 2 year sabbatical, crossing the Atlantic and cruising the Caribbean and Mediterranean seas, he's now an entrepreneur working in his passions.

Through his firm, Rising Tide Ventures, Matthew supports and mentors corporate escapees like himself, who are ready to pursue their own dreams and create something significant for themselves.

Join the revolution at:
www.risingtideventures.com.au/coworking-revolution
Share your insights, ideas and questions with other entrepreneurs:
www.facebook.com/risingtideventures
Twitter: @_risingtide
LinkedIn: au.linkedin.com/in/matthewdunstan

www.ingramcontent.com/pod-product-compliance
Lightning Source LLC
Chambersburg PA
CBHW022040190326
41520CB00008B/662